# Breaking Out

## of an
# Alabama Jail

*Life of a Sheriff's Daughter*

# Breaking Out

## of an
## **Alabama Jail**

*Life of a Sheriff's Daughter*

## Becky Horn Rogers

**AL**
PUBLISHING CO.
*Rutledge, Alabama*

Breaking Out of an Alabama Jail
Becky Horn Rogers
AtL Publishing Co.
Copyright  October 2024
ISBN- 9798342684118

*He will cover you with his feathers, and under his wings you will find refuge; his faithfulness will be your shield and rampart.*
Psalm 91:4 (NIV)

I believe in signs from above. My guardian angel, my mother, sends feathers. I find them in all sizes, in many places.

# Dedication

*This book is dedicated to my husband, Danny Rogers.*

*He has always offered steadfast support in every project I have undertaken.*

# Foreword

It's 6:08 a.m. on a Tuesday in late winter. I've been up almost two hours. Yes, I intentionally set my alarm for 4:30 a.m. I need, no, I cherish, this quiet time in our 1000 square foot condo. 72 years of thoughts, friendships, relationships, jobs, and just life must be recorded on paper for my family. And maybe a few friends or even strangers will find my upbringing fascinating. Some have told me just that and encouraged the writing of this autobiography.

A steady rain invites me to our balcony. My favorite chair cushion is wet so I spread my soft comfy blue and white throw over it. As I sit down with pen in hand I realize my paper is getting splattered just as the chair did. I pause for just a minute to feel the cool breeze. The palm fronds are waving good morning to me. I hear a sea

gull cawing as it passes by, then I retreat to my recliner.

The warm mug in my hands and the rich aroma of coffee conjure up by-gone days of my childhood. In this book I hope to share with my readers an experience like no other Baby Boomer I have ever known. You see, my father was the sheriff of Crenshaw County, Alabama and we lived in the Crenshaw County Jail.

# Special Thanks

Special thanks to:

- Jesus Christ for His unending love, patience, and grace

- Terrie McGhee Bedgood for an informative phone interview

- Bennie McDonald for an insightful interview

- Shirley McGhee for a healing phone conversation

- John Bozarth for floor plans of the jail

- Reverend Dr. Bob McKibben for proofreading

- Cousins, nieces, nephews, and Erin for sharing special memories

# My Family Tree

Michael Horn

Richard Whitehead Horn

George W. Horn

John H. Horn

Lennie F. Horn

Ray M. Horn

Rebecca Ann Horn Rogers

Erin Rebecca Rogers Jeffreys

/\

Coleman O'Neal Tranum     Anslee Rebecca Tranum

# Crenshaw County

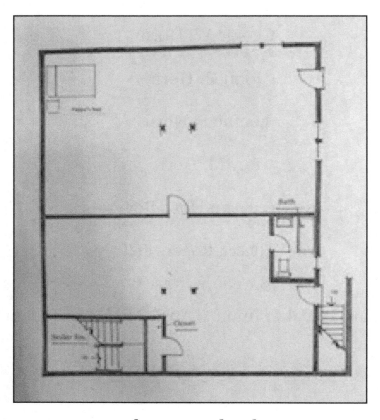

*basement level*

# Jail Floor Plans

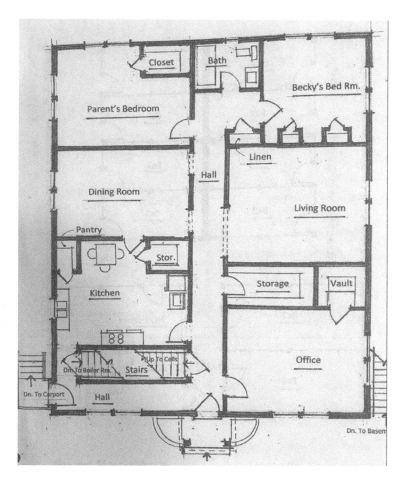

*our living area*

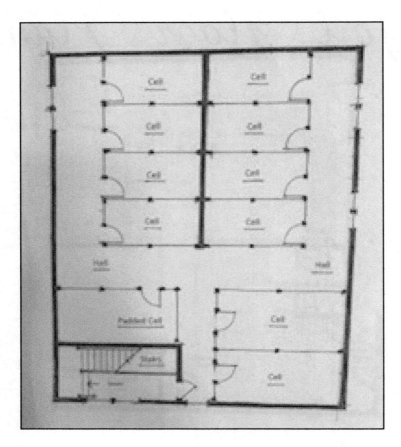

*upper level*

# Table of Contents

Forks in the Road ....................................................19

Horns-a-Plenty ..................................................... 23

Basement Recollections ..................................... 27

Unconditional Love..............................................31

Roots ...................................................................... 35

Elementary Years..................................................41

Junior High, High School,
  and the Tumultuous '60s ............................... 47

8th Grade..............................................................51

9th Grade..............................................................57

Sophomore Year...................................................61

Junior Year...........................................................65

A Dangerous Opportunity ................................ 69

Senior Year...........................................................73

Pictures .............................................................. 79

College ................................................................ 93

Marriage .............................................................. 95

The Honeymoon From Hell .............................. 99

My Mother, the Sheriff's Wife..........................101

My Daddy, the Sheriff.........................................105

Infertility, or Playing God? ............................. 109

Our Five Decade Love Story .............................111

Every Small Town Needs a Hero ...................... 121

Special Memories ...............................................125

My Cup Overflows...............................................139

"Southernese" - Common Southern
  Words and Phrases ...................................... 141

Afterword .............................................................143

# Chapter One
## Forks in the Road

*"When you come to a fork in the road, take it."-*
Yogi Berra

If you are a Baby Boomer (born between 1946-1964) you remember a March of Dimes poster child. Maybe it was an adorable little girl with curly blond hair and a frilly dress walking with the aid of crutches and leg braces. An Easter Seal poster child often posed while sitting in a wheelchair. I remember one chubby little boy in a striped shirt with a mischievous grin on his face. Had there been a poster child for Sheltered Children my face would have been on it. I often shouted to my mother, "I wish you had a dozen and couldn't keep up with any of us!" Looking back, I now realize growing up in Luverne, Alabama in the 1950s and 1960s was really an ideal, peaceful, safe experience for me.

As Yogi Berra advised, life is full of choices and we have to make those choices. A turning point in my young life was the result of a choice my parents made. From 1939, when my grandfather, Lennie Franklin Horn, was elected sheriff of Crenshaw County, Alabama until 1972 there was only one four year term when a Horn did not hold that position. After Papa Horn, and before Daddy,

Uncle Green Horn was sheriff. So the choice my parents made to occupy the family living quarters of the Crenshaw County Jail offered me experiences not many children have ever had.

I have vague recollections of living three other places in Luverne as a young child before we moved to the jail. We occupied the top left apartment of the quadruplex on First Street across from the Luverne Methodist Church. A small wooden house still stands on Fifth Street where I often played in the yard with Elaine Norsworthy. Edna Ruth, Elaine's mother, would come to visit and we played outside while our mothers talked. Elaine's favorite thing to do was pull my long ponytail until I cried. One day I went whining to Mama and Edna Ruth. Very emphatically Edna Ruth said, "Becky, I have spanked Elaine for the last time for pulling your hair. Next time she does it, pull hers back." So I did as I was told and that broke Elaine from ever pulling my hair again.

I have a few memories of a house we rented on Second Street. Brenda Jeffcoat was my next door neighbor and playmate. For the most part, we got along well. But occasionally she would make me mad and I'd go stomping back to my house yelling, "I'm never playing with that Brenda Jeffcoat again!" About an hour later I'd ask to go back to Brenda's. With a sly smile on her face, Mama would want to know if that was the same Brenda I was angry with an hour ago.

We were living in that house on Second Street when I got the only belt whipping I ever had. I don't remember why I was in trouble but when Mama got her switch after me I ran from her. Big mistake! Out the back door I went and around the house I sprinted with Mama after me. Pappy, Mama's father, was sitting on the front porch. As we rounded the front corner of the house he suggested Mama run faster or she would never catch me. I ran back into the house and hid under my bed. Second big mistake! Mama knew where I was but in her motherly wisdom remained calm and quietly said, "OK, Rebecca Ann, you'll have to come out sooner or later." She went about her daily chores and much later I slid out from under the bed. Mama and the belt were waiting. I never ran from her again.

We recently drove by the small white house on Second Street. Another memory came into focus about living in that location. The Stroud family lived in a house around the corner. Their house faced Forest Avenue. Mike had one of those big three-wheeled bikes. I wanted to ride that bike so one day I asked Mike if I could. He was willing to let me ride it - for a kiss! So at age five I kissed a boy for the first time and it was so worth it! I took off down the sidewalk on that bike with my long hair blowing in the breeze.

When I get to heaven I'm going to ask my parents if they got a stipend or bonus for living in the jail. I wonder if Mama got paid any salary for all those meals she cooked for the prisoners. Maybe it was rent free and that was an incentive to live there. But, oh my, what an experience it was to spend most of my childhood and all of my youth living in the Crenshaw County Jail!

# *Chapter Two*

## Horns-a-Plenty

*"To live in hearts we leave behind is not to die."*
- Thomas Campbell

One of my most valuable treasures is a book. Carolyn Horn Beck undertook the task to write *Horns-A-Plenty*. It was published in 1966. I was thirteen years old. This genealogy includes the descendants of Richard Whitehead Horn from 1801-1965. Richard Whitehead Horn and Rebecca Cox were married on November 3, 1825. This union was blessed with eight boys and six girls. George Horn was one of those eight boys. He was my great-great grandfather. Richard's father, Michael Horn, is briefly mentioned on page 2, thus I am a seventh generation Horn. That makes our daughter, Erin Rebecca Rogers Jeffreys an eighth generation Horn. Our grandchildren, Coleman O'Neal Tranum, and Anslee Rebecca Tranum (notice a family name of Rebecca) are ninth generation Horns.

As I write this autobiography we just held our 122nd Horn Reunion. It is always the third Sunday in July. For years it was held near Glenwood, AL at an open shed known as the Horn Shelter. Now we seek comfort in the air conditioned Glenwood Community Cenater. When a global pandemic began in 2020 we were determined to continue this tradition and held it outdoors for three years under the pavilion at Crenshaw County Lake. Because the Horn Reunion is the longest running consecutive family reunion in Alabama, I have invited *Southern Living* and Sean Dietrich (Sean of the South). Neither have shown up to write about us.

I can remember years when 100 -125 Horn descendants would spread the most delicious variety of home cooked foods on those wooden tables at the shelter. My Aunt Frances Horn Boswell brought glorified brownies and hid them under the table. She only gave those to relatives she liked. Thank goodness I was always one of the lucky recipients.

One wooden table stood perpendicular to the tables where the food was spread. This table held the book each person signed so that we had a record of attendance. Usually a small bouquet was placed by the book in memory of those gone on before us. A large metal washtub filled with ice cold water sat at the end of the table. We all drank from the same metal dipper and thought nothing of it!

Just like having our favorite church pew, we all had a desired place at a particular table to set up our tablecloths and food. In the opposite corner of the shelter were cousins we didn't know very well. One day in my late 40s I had a conversation with a co-worker who had married into that other corner but had since divorced.

I commented, "We used to call that corner where you were the fat corner." She quickly responded,"Well, they used to call y'all the rich corner!" We both got a good laugh from that conversation. We do love all our cousins and wish we saw more of each corner nowadays at the Horn Reunion.

For many years Mr. Sid Jackson wrote a column for the Luverne Journal called "Here and There." It was folded and yellowed but I found an article tucked away in my *Horns-A-Plenty* that was written around November or December of 1984. The title of that article was " Horn Name Integral Part of County History." The last paragraph of his article reads:

"On a recent Sunday we attended services at the Luverne Methodist Church. It so happened that there was a christening on that day, and the baby's name was Abigail Garrison. Abigail's mother is Angela Carpenter Garrison, whose mother is Jean Foster Carpenter. Jean's mother is Edna Kate Horn Foster, daughter of James W. Horn, son of James M. Horn, son of Richard Whitehead Horn, whose father was Michael Horn. Abigail represents the eighth generation. My God!

There must be thousands of them somewhere."

Abigail is the wife of our pastor, Dr. Jeremy Pridgeon, at First United Methodist Church - Panama City. I recently shared this article with her. Then later when she visited her grandfather, Clemont Carpenter, in Luverne he also shared the exact same article with her.

Through the years a standing joke has been if you bring your boyfriend/girlfriend or fiance to a Horn Reunion and he/she still marries you then it was meant to be.

### Horns a Plenty

We knew each year that it was time to go home from the reunion when our very short cousin, Jeanette O'Neal Veasey, began piling leftovers on several plates to take with her. Before political correctness we referred to her as a midget. My Aunt Frances didn't like her very much. Jeanette never got a glorified brownie!

# Chapter Three

## Basement Recollections

*"Some men can live up to their loftiest ideals without ever going higher than a basement."*
- Theodore Roosevelt

The jail had a walkout basement. The only way to go into the basement was to walk outside and enter using one of two doors. My Pappy, Charlie Clements, was my mother's daddy. Pappy was born September 23,1889. I never knew my mother's mother. Her name was Mary and she died May 15, 1947, five years before I was born. Pappy lived in the basement.

Pappy wore overalls. As a toddler (I am told) he would place my little bare feet in the hip pockets of his overalls and walk all around town with me tightly clinging to his neck. Years later we made those treks with me walking beside him tightly clinging to his callused hand. Our favorite stop was Mitchell Supply. This was a mercantile type store that sold just about anything one could imagine. Pappy and I would enter the front door and walk about half the length of the store to a bench that sat across from the cash register table. We would sit on that hard wooden bench enjoying hoop cheese, crackers, and

Coke or Pepsi in a glass bottle. Mr. Mitchell always took time to stop and visit with us. Before we left the store Pappy would buy a package or two of Stageplanks - those gingerbread flavored cookies with scalloped edges and pink frosting.

My entire family considers me nuts that I, now in my retirement years, get up at 4:30 a.m. to have my prayer time and devotional while holding a hot mug of strong black coffee. You see, that coffee aroma conjurs up my favorite basement memory. I would often spend the night with Pappy. He farmed as a sharecropper much of his life so he had to get up before dawn. Old habits are hard to break. We would wake up well before daylight. Pappy would have a pot of coffee ready and we would dip those Stageplanks in that coffee as we talked and laughed. I actually was drinking a little coffee in my milk. And of course, I was always allowed to go back to sleep. Pappy didn't have much as far as money or worldly possessions go but he had the gift of time for me. Those memories of our early morning basement days are more precious than any heirloom he could have left me.

Pappy surrendered his life to Christ on his death bed in that basement. He met Jesus face to face on December 16, 1964, at age 75. I was 12. In the book *Balcony People*, Joyce Landorf Heatherley writes insightfully about the gift and ministry of affirmation. She reminds us of those people in the balcony who shout words of encouragement to us. They motivate us to be what God intends for us. My Pappy was one of those balcony people living in the basement.

As I entered my teenage years, the vacant basement was the perfect place to host the best spend the night parties ever. One of the two rooms held four or five full size beds. So 8-10 teenage girls could stay up all night if we so desired - laughing, talking, and listening to the "drama queen" of the group cry over a boy. The first girl to fall asleep got her hand placed in a cup of warm water. We would wait patiently to see if this trick made her wet the bed. Soaking a bra in the bathroom sink then trying to put it on the sleeping owner without waking her was another silly thing we did. Occasionally, a group of 3-4 boys would come knocking on the basement door. We'd stand at the door and talk briefly but never let them in. I knew that would forever end our slumber parties if boys were caught in the basement.

When Danny and I married September 12, 1971 the basement became our first home. Danny was working at Super Foods and I was a full time student at Troy State University. His meager salary and my part-time job at Edna Ruth's Cloth Shop most likely qualified us at the poverty level. But we didn't care. We were young and in love. Finally gaining some independence from the sheltered life in which I had been raised, I felt like a free woman. I had literally gone from Mama to marriage. I loved living in that basement. We could come and go as we pleased. No curfew. I guess you could say I grew up while living where Pappy had lived.

Early one Saturday morning Danny left for work. His car was parked behind the jail near the basement entrance. He immediately reappeared and said, "You'd better call your daddy." Unbeknownst to us, in the middle of the night, two prisoners had located a crawl space, tied several sheets together, and shimmied down those sheets to freedom (they thought). The white sheets dangling near our bedroom window caught Danny's attention before he got in his car. The prisoners were soon caught and probably extended their stay at the Crenshaw County Jail. Despite true stories like this one, I was never afraid while living in the jail.

# Chapter Four

## Unconditional Love

*"Love is so unconditional; love liberates; love is the reason why I do what I do, and so I think it is the greatest gift we have."*
- BeBe Winans

Perhaps, if we are fortunate, we have three or four people in a lifetime that truly love us unconditionally. Bessie Ruffin Horn loved me unconditionally. We called her Cousin Bess and although I don't remember her husband, we referred to him as Uncle Jack. Uncle Jack was the son of James Horn. James was one of those fifteen children of the prolific Richard Whitehead Horn. Uncle Jack was born May 24, 1877. Cousin Bess was born May 6, 1882. They married November 4, 1901. According to our genealogy, *Horns-A-Plenty*, Uncle Jack was in the highway construction business back when mule teams and slip scrapes were used to move dirt. He was also in the grocery business in Luverne. In later years, he served as Justice of Peace in the Crenshaw County Courthouse. I wonder if he performed the marriage of my parents. I guess that will be one of those WISH (When I See Heaven) questions I'll ask. Uncle Jack died April 21, 1957.

## Unconditional Love

An old two story brick building stood at the corner of Glenwood Avenue and Sixth Street next door to the jail. We made reference to that structure as the old jail. I suppose it once housed prisoners and maybe even the sheriff's family. Cousin Bess lived on the first floor of that building so she was our next door neighbor. Cousin Bess was present when my one living grandmother was absent. I'll speculate on that in another chapter. So, like Pappy, all my memories of Cousin Bess are precious.

The old jail building was sort of creepy to me as a young girl but I loved visiting Cousin Bess because of the attention I received. Entering the front door, I faced a steep inside staircase, probably one that led to where the prisoners were housed years before. Mae and Clell Brook lived upstairs. They never used that staircase. They used an outside set of steep stairs. Their young adult daughter would drive up in her car, blow the horn, and down those steep stairs Mae would descend with JoAnn's freshly laundered and folded clothes in a big basket. Mama didn't dislike JoAnn but she disliked her action of letting her mother bring that heavy laundry basket down those dangerously steep metal stairs.

A long hallway led to Cousin Bess' two rooms where she lived. There was a small kitchen and a larger living room/bedroom. A small dimly lit bathroom sat at the end of the hallway, so exiting Cousin Bess' two room living space was necessary to get to the bathroom. The plaster on the walls of the hallway was badly cracked and peeling. I would often stop on my way in and peel it. The yellowed plaster would crumble in my hand and fall to the floor. Somehow I never got in trouble for that. Cousin Bess probably swept it up before Mama saw it. A room sat to the left about halfway down the hallway that I never remember anyone using. I suppose this was the formal dining room. It housed a beautiful oak dining table, six chairs, and a buffet (often referred to as a sideboard). The chairs have been replaced but the round oak table, which becomes an oblong table when two leaves are inserted, and the sideboard proudly give an eclectic look to our bayside condo today. I hope there is room for that furniture in my assisted living facility someday. When I do have to part with it I hope a Horn descendant wants it.

When I was old enough to spend the night with Cousin Bess she was well into her seventh decade. She always heated up Chef Boyardee spaghetti and meatballs and creamed corn for me. Lime or strawberry jello with whipped cream was dessert. After we ate at her small kitchen table we'd sit in the living room part of her bedroom and play games. We made up a game using pennies. If I cupped my hands together holding five pennies and Cousin Bess guessed seven she would have to give me two of her pennies. I'm not sure what happened if one of us underguessed the number of pennies each was holding.

It was common just before dusk to see bats circling above the Ford dealership across the street. Every once in a while one of those nasty bats would somehow get into Cousin Bess' house. A black bat swooping from wall to wall and just missing my head was a very unusual bedtime ritual. She didn't weigh a hundred pounds but she would grab her broom, swat that bat to the floor, hold it down with the broom, and beat it to death with a hammer. It's a miracle I could fall asleep or even return but I did both. After supper and the excitement of bat killing we would begin to prepare for bedtime. I would sit on the bench at Cousin Bess' vanity and brush my hair. She had a lovely gold brush and matching hand- held mirror. I thought the mirror was a magic one because my hair looked so pretty after I brushed it. Years later, I realized that mirror was actually covered in dust.

Cousin Bess' bedtime routine was to remove her dentures and place them in a cup of solution that sat on her bedside table. She would then pick up Uncle Jack's framed picture and kiss it twice. Always twice. I would crawl into bed and sleep on the inside near the wall. Cousin Bess always took the outside. Then what I really came to spend the night for commenced - back scratching. Every single time I slept over at Cousin Bess' she would scratch my back until I fell asleep. I'm in my seventies and Danny has to scratch my back every night. When Erin comes to visit or we are at her house, even in her forties, she usually makes her way next to me on the couch and says, "Mom, will you scratch my back?" And so the tradition continues.

On the night of November 6, 1973, I was playing bridge with a group of girlfriends. Mama knew where I was so she called there. She asked me to come immediately to the hospital. Just as I entered that silent hospital room Cousin Bess took her last breath at age ninety-one. A nurse appeared and Mama asked her to witness what happened next. Mama slipped Cousin Bess' silver filigree single diamond wedding ring off of her finger and onto mine.

# Chapter Five

## Roots

*"Families are like branches on a tree.
We grow in different directions yet our roots
remain as one."* Unknown

Lennie Franklin Horn was my grandfather I never knew. He was born August 2, 1891, and died July 9, 1947. He died the same year my grandmother that I never knew, Mary Clements, died. Papa Horn married Willie Annette Raley August 26, 1907. He had just turned 16. Mama Horn was 17. They must have conceived my daddy on their wedding night. He was born on May 29, 1908, the first of six children. They named my daddy Ray Minchener Horn. Minchener, a very unusual name, was the last name of the doctor who delivered Daddy. Their second child, Homer Green Horn, was born June 21, 1909. Annie Estelle Horn was born September 14, 1910. "Barefoot and pregnant" is a figure of speech most commonly associated with the notion that women should not work outside the home and should have many children during their reproductive years. Seems like Lennie and Willie were the epitome of "barefoot and pregnant." Mama Horn got a bit of a break and the fourth child, John Hayward Horn, was born September 16, 1915. Sara Frances Horn was born

March 21, 1917. The sixth child, Mary Elizabeth Horn, was born May 24, 1919.

My daddy's first wife was Muriel Elizabeth Franklin. Her nickname was "Lady." She was born November 8, 1912. They married November 20, 1927. She was 15. Daddy was 19. From that marriage three children were born. Willard Delwin Horn was born August 25, 1930. Dinah Ray Horn was born May 3, 1932. Genevieve (no middle name) was born April 10, 1936. On February 29, 1944, at age 31 Muriel was killed instantly in an automobile accident near Mobile, AL. My daddy, Mr. and Mrs. Edwin "Red" O'Neal, and Jack Beasley were also in the car. According to a newspaper article in The Luverne Journal Mr. and Mrs. O'Neal were seriously hurt and transported to a Mobile hospital. Mr. Beasley and my daddy received minor injuries. "Red" O'Neal was driving and Mr. Beasley was a front seat passenger. Through the years I was told that they were extraditing a prisoner from Mobile County to Crenshaw County so, if that is correct, Mr. Beasley was the prisoner since Mr. O'Neal was Daddy's cousin. It's interesting to me that Daddy took another couple with them instead of a deputy. We seldom talked about that wreck, but Dinah once told me that her mother had promised to make her a banana pudding when she got home.

I've referred to Mama Horn, Daddy's mother, as an absent grandmother to me. Perhaps she helped Daddy with his three motherless children and was worn out by the time I came along. My cousin, Susan Russell Reeves, shared a couple of memories from our childhood about Mama Horn. The years we remember her living in Luverne she had an apartment in the housing project known as Westdale Apartments. She kept a metal garbage can outside her back door. She would wash out egg shells, tin cans, and anything else that went into that garbage can so as to keep the raccoons and possums out of it at night. Mama Horn dipped snuff so when we would visit she would mix cocoa and sugar and let us put it between our gum and bottom lip to mimic her snuff habit. She loved to fish and fish alone so Daddy would give her a ride to the Crenshaw County Lake, drop her off, and pick her up before sunset. In the last years of her life, Mama Horn lived at Woodley Manor Nursing Home in Montgomery, AL and my mother and I would visit her every time we went shopping in Montgomery. Mama Horn died August 16, 1970.

On May 6, 1945 Daddy married Mable Guyneese Clements. Unusual names seemed to be the norm back then. Guyneese was 28. She had probably already been labeled a spinster. I've been told that at their first meal together Daddy told his three children that he knew Guyneese was not their mother and she was not there to take the place of their mother. But she was his wife and they would treat her with respect. They always did.

After several miscarriages, Mother gave birth to me on September 13, 1952. Delwin and Dinah were grown and gone. Genevieve "Genny" was 16. I always referred to them as my brother and sisters, not half siblings. I was my mother's only child and basically was raised as an only child since Genny left two years after I was born for Caraway Methodist Nursing School in Birmingham, AL. Dinah was already at Caraway. Here's another WISH question (When I See Heaven)- a question I wish I had asked growing up. Why were they allowed to go away to school but I wasn't? I'm sure I really did ask that question but never got a true answer. I suspect they got to the big city of Birmingham and sowed some wild oats!

## Roots

As a toddler, I adored Genevieve. She was beautiful. She had long very black hair. She played cymbals in the Luverne High School band so when I was big enough to play outside in the front yard I clanged two pot lids together and marched all around.

On July 19, 1956, when I was three years old, I became an aunt. Willie Ray Horn was born to Delwin and Martha. A few years later Stan was born. Ray and Stan called their grandfather Papa Horn and they called their grandmother Darlin'. A couple of weeks after Ray was born Dinah and Allen Hudson had my first niece, Nina Elizabeth. They went on to have Al and Madge. That set of grandchildren called their grandparents Papa Horn and Grandmama. Genevieve and Harry Weaver had Wade and Tim. Wade and Tim called their grandparents Papa Horn and Darlin', like Ray and Stan did. So my nieces and nephews were so close in age to me that they seemed like cousins and playmates when we were growing up. When our daughter, Erin, was born Daddy was deceased. Erin called my mother Nana. Mama had a daycare in her home. Through the years she kept dozens of children. They all called her Mama Horn, except for Kimberley Maddox. Kimberley heard the daycare kids say Mama Horn. She heard Erin say Nana. So all the years she was in daycare she called my mother Nana Horny!

Our roots run deep in Crenshaw County, AL and beyond. I have such fond memories as a child of my niece, Nina, coming for week long visits. They lived in Fort Payne, AL when Nina was young. Al and Madge never came to stay without their parents. Ray and Stan lived in Luverne so they were often around. Wade and Tim resided in Birmingham and they would also come for week long visits without their parents. Daddy and Mama managed to take each of the grandsons on trips to Alabama football bowl games. Once when Nina was visiting she was sitting cross-legged on the kitchen table. Mama was mixing lard, flour, salt, and whatever else went into those delicious homemade biscuits in a large wooden dough bowl. She would knead and knead then pinch off just the right amount of dough and roll it into a perfect biscuit. Nina asked, "Grandmama, what are you doing?" Mama replied, "Well, honey, I'm making biscuits." To which Nina responded, "That's not the way my mother does it. She just raps the can on the edge of the table!"

Ray was staying with us one day and was playing in the side yard. Mama looked out a window at the exact time Ray was dunking a tiny puppy of a new litter into a big washtub filled with water. She flew out the front door and down the outside stairs that led to the side yard. When Ray heard her yelling he threw the puppy down and ran. When Mama caught him he looked up at her and said, "Darlin' I didn't know you could run!" My guess is he didn't get a belt whipping. It is a miracle that I love Ray. Occasionally Mama and I would accompany him and his mother to visit Mama Franklin and Papa Franklin, Ray's paternal biological greatgrandparents (Daddy's first wife's parents). One afternoon during such a visit we were on the side porch of their country home. For some unknown reason Mama Franklin and Papa Franklin would put the cans they had used for spittoons on a low shelf of the porch. Ray picked up one of those cans half full of tobacco juice and poured it over my head. One can imagine the mess and the smell! Mama looked at Martha, Ray's mom, and emphatically said,"Martha, if you don't whip him I will." Of course, that visit was cut short to get me home and cleaned up.

I have two Horn cousins who also came for week long visits. To this day we remain close and call ourselves the Horn Sistas - the next generation. Donna is the daughter of Aunt Mary and Uncle "Boots" Alford. Mary Frances is the daughter of Aunt Frances and Uncle Frank Boswell. Donna is just a few months older than I am. Donna lived in Montgomery, AL so she was my city cousin. The first time I ever shopped at night was when I was at Donna's for a week one summer and we went to Gaylord's. I thought that was so cool to go out shopping at night. We also got to do fun and different outings like going to the recreation center at one of the junior high schools. Donna visited me one summer and went home recapping the week to Aunt Mary. After a few days, Aunt Mary called my mother and asked, "Guyneese, what in the world is Donna talking about? She says y'all went to this place and got wood and juice." After just a few moments my mother laughed and replied, "Oh, we went to the curb market and got sugar cane." It seemed the highlight of Mary Frances' visits to the jail was staying up late at night and eating Golden Flake potato chips and drinking Pepsi in bed. I guess Aunt Frances never allowed that.

We truly are the Horn Sistas - the next generation. Since we have no living parents, aunts, or uncles, we are the matriarchs of our families.

# Chapter Six

## Elementary Years

*"Your education is a dress rehearsal for a life that is yours to lead."*- Nora Ephron

Peepy and Pokey were my imaginary playmates. We spent hours together in the walk-in hall closet (labeled storage on the floor plan) playing all sorts of things. When I was a nurse like my sisters, they were my patients. When I was a teacher, they were my students. When I was a mom, they were my children. But when I began first grade they had to stay behind.

I loved elementary school. I enjoyed being around so many other children. Because the cut-off date for beginning school was October 1, I entered first grade about two weeks before my sixth September 13 birthday. I was one of the youngest in my class. Not fun when I wanted my driver's license but amusing now when they all hit a new decade before I do.

There was no public school kindergarten in the 1950s. There was a private kindergarten in town but Mama was working at a factory and Dadddy was a guard in Montgomery at the state capitol building that year so I had no way to get to and from kindergarten. And besides, we probably could not have afforded it.

## Elementary Years

My first grade teacher was Mrs. Oleta Petrey. Little did I realize that school year that I was in the room with a few people who would become life-long friends. What six year old thinks about that? We had a hula hoop contest one day and Petricia Kettler won. She got a whole wrapped package of chewing gum donated by Petrey Wholesale. I think it was 12 or 24 packs of gum. That was probably the first time I ever felt jealous of anyone.

There was one tiny girl in our class who came from a large family. I had outgrown a pretty pair of white patent leather shoes with small plastic pastel flowers on top. Mama sent me to school with those shoes to give to that classmate. I cried. That was my earliest recollection of generosity and compassion.

We were not allowed in first grade to count on our fingers. I was doing just that with my fingers under my desk when Mrs. Petrey walked by and asked, "Becky, are you counting on your fingers?" "No, ma'am," was my quick reply. I knew I had lied and broken a school rule and was so upset when Mama got home from work. She saw that I would not rest until we called Mrs. Petrey and I told the truth and apologized. Honesty was a trait I learned at a very young age.

My hair was long and hung down my back, usually in ringlets Mama had somehow created. I was very tender-headed as a little girl. Mama would brush and style my hair before going to work at the slacks factory and I would scream and cry. She got so tired of that morning routine. So by the spring of first grade she had my hair all whacked off. And to add to that I had impetigo on my chin. My first grade school picture was hideous!

### Breaking Out of an Alabama Jail!

Second grade was a memorable year for sure. Mrs. Georgia Summerlin was my teacher. She was a wonderful teacher and a kind, compassionate, flexible human being. I contracted hepatitis during my second grade year. I remember Mama placing her ironing board at the foot of my bed and while she ironed I complained about how awful I felt. When we got to Troy to Dr. J.O. Colley's office he took one look at the whites of my eyes, which by then, were yellowed, and diagnosed hepatitis. He insisted that Mama and Daddy take the shot, then sent me straight to Edge Memorial Hospital where I stayed for a week. Mama never left my bedside. Each morning when the nurse entered my room with that painful B12 shot I would cry before she ever touched me. One particular morning I had made up my mind I would be brave. I didn't cry at all. Mama rewarded me with a little wind up carousel.

During that hospital stay I learned about the emotional and physical strength of a mother. One night a male patient went crazy and was pacing the hallway screaming. Mama shoved a large metal dresser against my hospital room door to protect me from that man.

Pappy and Mrs. Summerlin had to take the shot that prevents contracting hepatitis because they had been in close contact with me. I'm thankful my classmates didn't have to take it because they would have probably hated me for that. I remember being welcomed back to my second grade classroom after a lengthy absence.

My third grade teacher was Mrs. Christine Mooney. She was kind and easy going. Her husband, Hugh Mooney, was our principal. He would find us on the playground and push us around and around on that spinning apparatus. He always wore a suit and tie but he could get us going fast as we stood on the platform and held on for dear life to the metal bars.

I began taking piano lessons in third grade. Mrs. Roberta Little was my teacher. I took for eight years. Usually, my piano lesson took place before school in the little block building near the football stadium.

One of the boys in my third grade class taught me a new four-letter word. I came home asking Mama what it meant and she loudly told me to never let that word come out of my mouth again. She never gave me the definition. (Hint: it began with an f.)

Fourth grade was my very favorite year of elementary school. Mrs. Mary Gardner was my teacher. She was one of the kindest people I have ever known. One day she could see I was struggling on a science test. I was trying to think of some use for some type of rock, maybe marble or limestone. She leaned over and whispered to me,"Have you ever been to a cemetery?" So I got that answer of a grave headstone correct.

Mama made all my clothes including my pajamas. One morning in my haste to get ready for school I forgot to pull off the bottoms of my baby doll pajamas. I didn't realize I had them on until I went to the bathroom located right next door to Mrs. Gardner's classroom. I was mortified! I went back into the classroom and whispered to Mrs. Gardner what I had discovered. She assured me nobody but the two of us would know unless I told my friends.

During one of my elementary education courses at Troy State University we were challenged to write about our favorite teacher. I wrote about Mrs. Gardner and mailed her a copy.

Good thing I had kind, sweet-spirited teachers in grades one through four. I can't say that about fifth grade. Mrs. Madie Horn was mean. Just mean. She was the mother of Carolyn Horn Beck who wrote *Horns-A-Plenty*, thus a distant cousin to us by marriage. Her husband was Felix Horn. She slapped Warren Jackson one day in front of the whole class. I can't remember what the issue was but once she realized he was right and she was wrong she did apologize to him in front of the class. She would put me in the hall for talking too much. Imagine that! I'd stand there and pray the principal would not walk by. That whole school year I wondered why I didn't get Mrs. Maurine Walker as a teacher. She was the mother of my best school friend, Lynann. Death paid a visit to our grade that year when we lost Johnny Cornett in an automobile accident.

Sixth grade was also a part of elementary school in the 50s and 60s. There was no middle school. Mrs. Audrey King was my teacher. I loved her. She read *Ivanhoe* aloud to us. All through my career as an educator, my favorite part of each school day was reading aloud to my students.

On November 22, 1963, I had been to a piano lesson during the school day instead of before school. As I returned to Mrs. King's classroom, I learned the awful news that President John F. Kennedy had been assassinated in Dallas. Those scenes in the days to follow of his motorcade, Dealey Plaza, Jackie Kennedy, and John John saluting his daddy's casket will be forever seared in my mind.

## Elementary Years

I had my first boyfriend in sixth grade. Keith Jay-roe and I would be paired up at parties to play Penny Go Walking. Someone would walk around the room with two pennies. We cupped our hands and the boy and girl who got the pennies went walking outside in the dark. Keith recalls I was the first girl he ever kissed.

Our sixth grade dance was held in the school gym. The decorations were simple red and white crepe paper streamers woven together and draped from the rails along the top level of the gym. Mama made my outfit. It was a reddish colored shift dress of kettle cloth fabric and I wore a white short sleeve top under it. I wore a white stretch headband. There were sixty-eight students in that picture which I still have today. I never dreamed the girl sitting to my right would be killed in a car crash a few years later.

# Chapter Seven

## Junior High & High School

### The Tumultuous '60s

*"A child's life is like a piece of paper
on which every person leaves a mark."*
- Chinese Proverb

There was no term middle school in the 1960s. We went from elementary to junior high. In our 1965 yearbook, Panorama, we were classified as the Junior One class (7th graders). Freshmen were known as Senior Ones. I wonder if a small country school or two in the county closed around this time. There were 98 students pictured in our seventh grade class, 30 more than the year before.

Mr. C.W. Claybrook was our principal. He drew an imaginary line in the hallway outside the school office. Junior high students (7th-9th) were to stay on one end of the hallway. Senior high students (10th-12th) were to remain on the other side of the line on their hallway of classrooms.

In 7th grade I learned from Mrs. Sara Capps that it is a woman's prerogative to change her mind. Oh, how many times I have used that quote! As I recalled the faculty members I had that year, I realized, unbeknownst to me, that I was learning how to treat and how to not treat my future students.

Mr. Lowell Carter, ag teacher, and I had an innocent bet of a whole quarter (25 cents) over the Alabama-Auburn football game that fall. Bama won and when I boasted about the quarter I won my mother loaded me into her car and drove me to Mr. Carter's house on Forest Avenue. Humiliated, I had to knock on his door and return the coin. I'm just thankful Mama didn't walk me to the door and give him a piece of her mind.

I didn't know many of the senior high girls but one of them in particular made an impact on me. Nancy Hettinger, a blonde beauty, signed my yearbook with these words,"Lots of luck to a real sweet girl. Remember 1st year P.E. Love ya, Nan" I'm not sure why a high school junior and a 7th grader shared a P.E.class unless she was Mrs. Catherine Norman's helper.

I loved Mrs. Norman. She was the mom of my classmate, Butch. She was beautiful and because she was our summer lifeguard at the city pool she had a gorgeous tan. I always enjoyed P.E. but was a little intimidated when Mrs. Norman would shout, "I'll snatch your arm off and beat you with the bloody end of it!" She never did.

I was probably one of the few kids who looked at the section in the back of the yearbook where locals had purchased advertisements. My daddy bought a half page ad. I was proud to see his picture as he was standing in his office at the courthouse in his sheriff's uniform. I do not remember this attire. I always remember him dressed in a suit, hat, and tie with a clip tie pin. One of the items that caught my eye in this ad was a hand grenade used as a paper weight.

After the courthouse closed for the day, Daddy and several local gentlemen would gather in a room in the basement of the courthouse for a game of dominoes. If I ever had an occasion to interrupt their game (which didn't please my daddy) I would enter the unlocked back door of the courthouse and descend a few stairs. That's where I would see the two restroom doors. One was labeled "Whites Only". The other was labeled "Colored Only".

Living in the Crenshaw County Jail, I saw and heard things in the 1960s that most young people never even thought about. Occasionally the unrest of that decade would result in activists visiting our county and getting arrested.

Mama always said there was a big difference between a woman and a lady. A rather large African American woman was brought into the jail. Each prisoner was fingerprinted in the room to the right of the front door used as an office. The fingerprint kit with the messy black ink was set up on Mama's large chest freezer. Before being locked up, she had to be frisked by my mama. Mama confiscated an ice pick from her full-figured bosom. That ice pick remains in one of my kitchen drawers today.

1965 was a year of heightened racial tension. The Selma to Montgomery marches for voting rights of black citizens took place that year. Viola Liuzzo was a civil rights activist from Detroit, Michigan. On March 25, 1965 she was driving other activists between Selma and Montgomery and was shot and killed. She left behind five children.

I remember hearing the comment, "Well, if she had been home with her children where she belonged that wouldn't have happened." As I grew into maturity, I realized brave women like her helped to change the world.

I was not an activist nor a protestor in seventh grade. I just remember thinking how close all that unrest was to my Aunt Nelia (Mama's sister) and my Uncle R.L.Seekers who lived in Selma. My self-absorbed mind could only think about how I wanted to continue my week long visits there in the summer where they doted on me because they had no children.

Many will find it hard to believe but I got my last doll while I was in 7th grade. She was a walking doll dressed in pink. I held her hand and as I walked, her legs moved also. As my 7th grade year came to a close, I started thinking about holding hands with boys, not a doll.

# Chapter Eight

## Eighth Grade (Junior II)
### The Tumultuous '60s

*"Our constitution is color-blind, and neither knows nor tolerates classes among citizens. In respect of civil rights, all citizens are equal before the law. The humblest is the peer of the most powerful."*
John Marshall Harlan,
Dissenting Opinion, Plessy v. Ferguson

Just before my eighth grade year began, my parents and I took a long vacation. We were in Anaheim, California visiting Disneyland at the time of the Watts riots. These confrontations between city police and residents of Watts and other predominantly African American neighborhoods of Los Angeles began on August 11, 1965. At the motel where we were staying, we met a family who had to seek refuge there because the fires had gotten so hot and so dangerous near their home.

Civil unrest seemed to be nationwide. As Daddy pulled into the semi-circle drive in front of Luverne High School to drop me off, a few Ku Klux Klan members were marching on the lawn. That was scary! I remember thinking that these men might be identified by their shoes. That was the only thing visible since the rest of each man was covered in a white robe and hood. I can only imagine the fear the few African American students felt that came to Luverne High School that year as partial integration was underway.

The only person I knew with a skin color other than mine was Monk. I never knew her real name. I'm not sure she even knew her birthdate. Oh how I loved Monk and she loved me. She had the softest lap. She helped my mama at the jail. Monk would stand over that big black six burner stove and cook some good Southern food. She would set up the ironing board in the office room and sit on a stool to iron. For some reason, that position drove my mama crazy. She couldn't understand anyone sitting to iron. It might have been because everything was ironed including my daddy's boxer shorts and handkerchiefs. Year later, when Monk got sick Mama was the one who ministered to her with visits and food.

Up until eighth grade I knew no black children. I knew no Hispanics. I knew no Koreans. I only knew white children.

Shirley McGhee was in my eighth grade class. Her skin was a dark mahogany and her black hair was short and curly. Mrs. Ann Mitchell gave us a vocabulary Social Studies homework assignment. She called on Shirley to share the meaning of monopoly (as in a single seller or producer of an item or service). When Shirley responded, "A game played on a board, " the whole class laughed. Shirley, I'm so sorry I laughed. Wherever you are today please accept my apology. She must have felt so lonely and isolated.

*Breaking Out of an Alabama Jail!*
*(author's note): I got in touch with Shirley via her sister, Terrie McGhee Bedgood, and on June 19, 2024, we had a phone conversation in which I personally apologized to Shirley.*

This school year I had a crush on Bobby Owens who was a Senior Two (Junior). His days were spent on the other side of that imaginary hallway line. Somehow we passed in the hallway and he spoke. Breathless and flustered, I could hardly speak as I told my girlfriends about this brief encounter.

Writing on the blank back pages of our yearbook was a big deal. Some wrote sincere wishes and some wrote silly ones. Here are a few from my Panorama:

* Good luck to a really cute girl. May you always have the best life has to offer.
Love ya,
GoGo


* Remember the M
Remember the E
But most of all
Remember ME!
Ronnie Uptain

To one of the nicest cousins a girl could have.
Love ya lots,
Susan Russell


I wish Bobby had signed my yearbook.

## Eighth Grade (Junior II)

My eighth grade year was the year my protective parents began allowing me a little freedom. I enjoyed being a member of the Pep Squad and riding the bus to out of town football games. We knew every word of "Teen Angel" and "Last Kiss." To stay awake, we sang "99 Bottles of Beer on the Wall."

In the 1960s, spring break was known as A.E.A. Teachers had a week off and could attend the Alabama Education Association conference. Two of our teachers planned educational trips instead of going to the conference. On March 12, 1966, Mrs. Susie Petrey and Miss Rachel Lightfoot accompanied 46 LHS students to Washington, D.C., Williamsburg, and Mount Vernon. Of course, my mother was a chaperone, but that was such a fun trip.

Just before we exited the bus at our D.C. hotel 'Miss' Susie gave us a few last minute instructions/rules. Out of an abundance of caution, she told us to not tell anyone we were from Alabama. She didn't want others to associate us with the civil rights unrest. And she didn't want others labeling us country bumpkins. Nice hotels had elevator operators. So as a few of us entered the elevator with our luggage the elderly African American gentleman dressed in his uniform asked us what floor we wanted and where we were from. 'Miss' Susie's son, Joe, shouted, "We're from Selma, Alabama!"

We had a marching band but Daddy told me the only way I could participate would be if they let me roll a piano on the field on wheels. Genevieve got to march in the band, but not me. So while cheering for the LHS tigers from the stands, I became interested in trying out for cheerleader. At the end of my eighth grade year I tried out, dancing a pom-pom routine to "These Boots Are Made For Walk-ing." I was elected 'B' team cheerleader.

Daddy's half page ad in the 1966 Panorama showed him sitting at his desk with neatly stacked papers and large bound records of some sort. He was dressed in the familiar suit, hat, and tie. Daddy used an old black Royal manual typewriter. He often referred to his typing as the HPC method - hunt, peck, and cuss.

# Chapter Nine

## Ninth Grade

### The Tumultuous'60s

*"That's where the future lies, in the youth of today."-*
Willie Stargell

Freshman year I was getting closer to that imaginary line into the world of high school. Dating for me at that time meant sitting on the couch on Sunday night in the living room of the jail holding hands and watching "Bonanza" or going out with a boy and his family. I had a bigger crush on Michael Landon (Little Joe Cartwritght) than I did on Bobby Owens.

While most of us were enjoying the innocence of our youth, many boys were shipping off to Vietnam. Several Crenshaw County young men served our country well. Most came home, but never to be the same. There were no cable news networks nor 24 hour news channels so my friends and I went about our self-interested days of school, clubs, cheering, sports, and church activities.

Two inscriptions that I am particularly fond of in my 1967 Panorama are:

To a very nice girl and a good friend.
Danny Rogers


To one of the greatest and best friends a person could have

Please stay just as you are.
P.S. I want another date.
Love,
Kline

Kline Jeffcoat was my first steady boyfriend. One night we went someplace with his parents and his younger brother, Ronnie. When Mr. Max drove up in front of the jail Kline said, "Okay, see'ya." 'Miss' Edna whirled around from the passenger front seat and shrieked, "Kline Jeffcoat, you get out of this car and walk her to the door!" He obeyed.

Today Kline and Patsy Petrey Jeffcoat have been married 50+ years and are our good friends. We enjoy playing bunko together and occasionally watching Alabama football games in their Panama City Beach home.

Isn't life interesting? Danny Rogers, still a man of few words, and I just celebrated 53 years of marriage.

Douglas Sanders was in the Junior Two (Eighth grade) class during the 1966-67 school year. He was an African American boy with very short hair and prominent ears. In Luverne, we could only get three television stations. One of those stations was Channel 4 WTVY out of Dothan, Alabama. So Douglas got the nickname "Channel 4" due to his ears. Kids compared his ears to rabbit ears which often sat on a television set for better reception. While I never called him that to his face I'm sure I referred to him as "Channel 4" instead of Douglas. Douglas, I'm so sorry we did that to you. Wherever you are today, please accept my apology. He must have felt so lonely. Kids were cruel, even back then.

P.S. Kline broke up with me the summer after my freshman year.

# Chapter Ten

## Sophomore Year
### The Tumultuous'60s

*"The future belongs to those who believe in the beauty of their dreams."*- Eleanor Roosevelt

My love of writing began my sophomore year when I became a member of the Creative Writing Club. We published a booklet, "Quill Craftsmen Quotes" that was composed primarily of creative works by Luverne High School as well as Luverne Elementary School students. Mrs. Jean Petrey was our sponsor. I was also a member of the "Tiger Rag" staff. That was our school newspaper.

The groundwork for my career as a teacher instead of a nurse must have been laid during the 1967-68 school year. I joined Future Teachers of America (FTA). Our chapter was the largest in its five year history at LHS. Mrs. Betty Speed and Mrs. Jean Petrey were our sponsors.

Perhaps because of lack of interest, our LHS band no longer existed. So under the leadership of Mrs. Pat Folmar, Mrs. Lucy Jackson, and Mrs. Glenda Head a drill team was formed. We were The Tigerettes. We performed at basketball games, football games, and in the beauty pageant program.

My favorite activity my sophomore year was choir. Jim Head was such a fun teacher/choir director. We had 98 members and rated superior at state competition. I was also part of a smaller ensemble of 16 known as The Serenaders. Mr. Head wanted the male athletes to be a part of choir. He had them try out and ran the scale on the piano as each one sang "Do, Re,Mi..." When he heard tone deaf Danny Rogers sing Mr. Head muttered, "Uh, maybe you could drive the bus."

What I liked least of all in senior high school was the selection process for beauty pageant participants. The entire class would gather in a classroom and several girls would be nominated to represent our class in the annual beauty pageant. Only four could be selected by popular vote. One of the boys would nominate the most homely girl in our class and snicker, along with his immature friends, as he did so. So those of us nominated would stand in the hall while the class selected four beauties. This was humiliating to the homeliest girl and embarrassing to the rest of us nominated but never chosen. We felt like a few gray pigeons among a muster of beautiful peacocks as we entered the room to learn the voting results.

Once the disappointment of not being a beauty dissipated, I enjoyed being in the variety program portion of the beauty pageant. The 1967-68 theme was "World of Color." The Serenaders sang with the girls perched on stools and the boys standing behind us.

Handsome senior, Danny Rogers, was one of eight

chosen as Senior High Favorites. He was involved in 4-H, Future Farmers of America (FFA), L Club, beauty pageant programs, football, basketball, Who's Who, and Class Giftorian. Fifty-eight seniors were pictured in the 1968 *Panorama*. Danny Rogers was my steady boyfriend. On the night he graduated I cried.

There were rules for dating the sheriff's daughter.

• Never drive up and blow the horn. She will not be allowed to come out.

• Get her home by or before curfew.

• If you don't get her home by curfew, don't come back.

• Only come "courting" when a parent is home (almost always at the jail).

• Stay on your side of the car at the drive-in movie.

• Always have on socks and a shirt when you come inside to "court".

One night Mama and Daddy had gone to bed and Danny and I were sitting on the couch watching television. We could sit close enough on the couch to hold hands. There was no rule about sitting a few feet apart on the sofa. The prisoners began to get loud and chanting commenced. Danny looked at me and stated, "Your daddy will be in here in a few minutes." Sure enough Daddy walked through the living room in his boxer shorts and wife beater undershirt with his billy club in hand. In his very slow Southern drawl he looked at us and said, "I'll be back in a few minutes." Up the stairs he went and he

63

took care of the late night disturbance. As he passed back through the living room, billy club still in hand, he looked at Danny and suggested, "Son, don't you think it's about time you go home?" "Yes, sir!", Danny replied and got out of there without even a good night kiss. (That billy club is housed in my nightstand today.)

In 1968 "Sloop John B" was released by The Beach Boys. My classmate, John Brooke, enjoyed coming to the jail where we would play that record on my stereo in the living room and make up pom-pom routines. Weird!

Daddy bought an old 1953 Ford clunker from a lady in town. It would get me across town (5 minute drive) to Edna Ruth's Cloth Shop on Saturdays where I began working for $5.00 per day.

# Chapter Eleven

## Junior Year
### The Tumultuous '60s

My junior year I was inducted into the Sapiens Chapter of the National Honor Society. We had a formal ceremony in the LHS auditorium. Then on May 7 we went to Mrs. Sara Folmar's backyard for an informal initiation. We new members dressed as storybook characters and crawled around singing "for we are jolly good Sapiens." There was some gross stuff we were made to eat. I especially remember the canned dog food.

FTA, Tiger Rag staff, pep squad, glee club, drill team, and creative writing club were all a part of my junior year. Title IX went into law in 1972 so I missed female organized sports by a few years. I'm sure I would have been part of a girls' basketball team or a girls' softball team, or both.

Our beauty pageant theme was "Let Us Entertain You." We opened the program singing, "Let us entertain you, let us make you smile," as we entered from the back of the auditorium wearing white oil cloth overcoats belted at the waist and a few inches above the knee.

## Junior Year

Junior year was so much fun. We transformed the gym and cafeteria into a "Holiday in Acapulco" and entertained the seniors at the Junior-Senior prom.

While my friends and I enjoyed decorating the gym the night before prom, Danny and other young men were in Montgomery, Alabama at the induction center for draftees. Young men between the ages of 18 and 25 were sent out induction notices from the Selective Service System. Danny's draft number was 2. His serious football knee injury and his being color blind classified him as F4 and kept him out of Vietnam. Needless to say, on May 2, 1969, we had something to celebrate in addition to prom.

Most teenagers do stupid things. The night of our junior class party we did a most foolish antic. We had purchased spray paint (mostly red, some white) and decided we were going to paint the town. I'm sure our sponsors got a little suspicious when many of us left the party at the same time. The next morning the town woke up to read "Class of '70" almost everywhere they turned. A few boys had climbed the steep metal steps of the water tower and painted "Class of '70" in large letters. Some culprits did the same on the mail box receptacle outside the post office which was federal property. The sheriff's daughter was guilty of spraying "Class of '70" on the street right in front of LHS.

On Monday morning the whole junior class was called together. Mr. Claybrook and Coach Sport, one of our sponsors, wanted to know who did what. As I recall, nobody spoke up that day. However, either one at a time, or in small groups, we eventually confessed. It's a miracle I wasn't locked up in my own home! So a few weeks later on a Saturday morning we gathered on the sidewalk outside the police department with our fine of a few dollars in hand and somehow cleaned up our mess.

A few months before my junior year the world was still in turmoil. Dr. Martin Luther King, Jr. was assassinated at the Lorraine Motel in Memphis, Tennessee on April 4, 1968. While we heard about such far-reaching events as Dr. King's murder and the 1963 Birmingham church bombing that killed four young black girls, we never dreamed life-altering events were taking place close to home.

The next chapter is one family's personal account of such an event.

# Chapter Twelve

## A Dangerous Opportunity

*"One brush stroke stands for danger;*
*the other for opportunity.*
*In a crisis, be aware of the danger -*
*but recognize the opportunity."*
- John F. Kennedy

Joseph McDonald was the first African American to graduate from Luverne High School. He was a member of the Class of 1969. Joseph first came to LHS for the 1965-66 school year.

In an interview with me, Joseph's older brother, Bennie, recalled what life was like for Joseph and his family during that time.

These are Bennie's words:

"Mama called me aside and told me Daddy had signed Joe up to go to Luverne High School. I didnt want to go because I was a senior at Woodford Avenue School."

"Black families could apply in the summer for LHS and the Board of Education would let them know who was accepted. We weren't paid by anyone nor any organization. We just wanted to be pioneers who helped to open the door to integration."

"Joe was afraid but he was brave. For a few weeks after the school year started, when Joe got home and we asked how his day went he would answer 'just fine.' He finally broke down one afternoon and started telling us how it really was. A white bully had begun kicking Joe. This went on for a while.

Finally, Mrs. Trubie Merle Strickland, LHS math teacher, saw it happen and took the bully to the principal's office."

"The bully was expelled and not too long after that I was home with the flu. I heard a loud car coming down our dirt road and a couple of shots rang out. I ran out on the porch and a shot whizzed by my head. He turned the car around a little piece down the road and came back and shot again. My daddy and I got the FBI involved after that incident. A couple of days later, we went to see Sheriff Horn.

We felt his reaction was rather casual which led us to believe he knew about the shooting episode. Not long after that the guy and his car disappeared."

"Joe passed away in 2009. In 2010 I decided Joe should be honored with a plaque in the trophy case that stands in the hallway of LHS. A program was held in the LHS auditorium to a packed house where the plaque and Joe's history were revealed. Martha Morgan and Lois Turner Truss, both members of the LHS Class of 1968, were instrumental in helping with this program and in helping me establish a scholarship in Joe's memory. A $500 scholarship is given each year to a graduating senior of Luverne High School. Essays are written and the winner is selected by a committee. The title of the Essay is " How I Have Persevered in Light of Social Hardships."

The scholarship fund is at First Citizens Bank and anonymous donations are made."

"I'd say kids of both races, white and black, were sheltered back then. I'm proud my parents were pioneers of integration. I'm just glad they let me stay where I was."

Bennie sat down with me at a Luverne restaurant and we talked further about those years. WSFA Channel 12 in Montgomery ran a segment on the presentation of Joseph's plaque. Bennie shared with me, via a DVD, the piece that WSFA aired. Terrie McGhee Bedgood was interviewed following the ceremony and her statement voiced those trying times so well. She said, "We were all children and we were all trying to survive."

Thank you, Bennie McDonald, for sharing with me and for your 20 years of service to our country in the United States Air Force.

# Chapter Thirteen

## Senior Year

*"There will come a time when you think everything is finished. That will be the beginning."*
- Louis L'Amour

I tried out for varsity cheerleader as my junior year came to an end and was elected. Mrs. Pat Folmar was our sponsor. 'Miss' Pat took five of us to Tuscaloosa, Alabama for summer cheerleader clinic at the University of Alabama. For three days we worked diligently in the heat to learn new cheers and pom-pom routines and loved every minute of it. One night we almost missed curfew and came within about two minutes of getting locked out of the dorm that housed us. 'Miss' Pat also took us on a beach trip. That was the only way I could go to the beach without my parents.

One night we were cheering at a basketball game. Our gym was old and the wooden bleachers were hard and worn. We all had to scoot over to make room for someone and as we did Sue Kendrick got a very large splinter in her lower butt cheek. There was no way we could get that thing out so Sue and I walked to her home on Sixth Street where her daddy, a doctor, extricated it and we walked back to finish our cheering duties.

JoAnne Holland represented our class well as homecoming queen. Sherry Kent was selected Miss Football for the second year in a row. Senior class president, Steve Nichols, welcomed the class of 1960 during our homecoming festivities. Then the student body was addressed by Guthrey Jeffcoat, class of '60 president. Fun-filled days like that will be forever etched in our memories.

Sometimes things are etched in one's memory that you wish would go away. My daddy loved Alabama football and took all the grandsons, usually two at a time, to bowl games. He and Mama took my first cousin, Donna Alford, and me to Dallas, Texas to the Cotton Bowl. Out of character for protective Mama, one morning she suggested that Donna and I browse through the brochures in the motel lobby of all the attractions in Dallas. She left us in the lobby and told us to stay there and she would return for us. After a while we got bored and returned to the room. They had hooked the chain but forgot to actually lock the door. When I abruptly opened the door about four inches what I saw will be forever etched in my mind! I knew they had done that once to get me here, but on vacation. Seriously?

Our beauty pageant on April 3, 1970, was themed "Sights and Sounds of the Sixties." Lee Jackson, LHS junior, was choreographer and her numbers helped us travel through the sixties in song and dance. A small group of us danced to The 5th Dimension's "Aquarius (Let the Sunshine In)". 50+ years later I can still recall a few moves to that dance number.

*Breaking Out of an Alabama Jail!*

Once again 'Miss'Susie organized an educational tour. We visited Williamsburg, VA, Washington D.C., and New York City. The visits to the U.S. Senate and House galleries while Congress was in session were an added bonus.

The organized talents of a few served to represent the school as a whole. As a feature editor of the *Panorama*, I helped create a biography of our senior year.

As I approached young adulthood, I began thinking about one day being married and not sheltered. Owning a hope chest was common. It was gradually filled with household items collected through the years. So my senior year I added a place setting of sterling silver to my cedar chest. The place setting was awarded to me for winning the Sterling Silver Homemaker Award. Miss Teresa Zeladonis presented it to me at the FHA banquet. She was our home-ec teacher when Mrs. Linda Bland was on maternity leave with twins. Danny's sister, Jeanice, found that award amusing since I didn't even know how to make sweet tea.

Edna Ruth's Cloth Shop bought a whole page ad in the 1970 yearbook. I'm pictured cutting fabric while three classmates look on. By this time I was making $10.00 for all day Saturday. I would take a couple of dollars next door to Marjorie's Homemakers Shop and pay down on some special treasure I had placed on layaway for my hope chest.

My first published writing appeared in the senior class section of the *Panorama* called "A Graduation Happening." We lost Johnny Cornett in an automobile accident during elementary school. Lesa Kay May had moved to an adjoining county but stayed in touch with her best friend, Susan Russell. Lesa Kay, at age 16, was on her way to visit Susan when she was killed in a car crash.

## A Tribute to Two Deceased Members of the Graduating Class of 1970

Two members of the Class of '70
Won't be with us, come this May,
For they'll be watching from their heavenly home,
On our graduation day.

With their gowns of purest white
And their cords of brilliant gold,
They'll sing with us the Alma Mater
While the other angels behold.

One cold day in 1962
The news began to spread;
There's been a terrible accident
And children, Johnny's dead.

With her laughter and her smile
And the beauty of her face,
God called Lesa home with Johnny
To take her heavenly place.

Someday the Class of '70
Will all be together again.
We'll join with Lesa and Johnny
in the mansion that God has planned.

Becky Horn

*Breaking Out of an Alabama Jail!*

On May 4, 1970, four unarmed college students were killed on the campus of Kent State University by the Ohio National Guard. A rally was being held to protest the expanding involvement of the Vietnam war into Cambodia. The students were also protesting the National Guard presence on campus and the draft. Watching segments of those protests on television was very disturbing to me.

The Luverne High School Class of 1970 was the last class to graduate before full integration of Crenshaw County Schools.

# Photos

*From cute pre-school age*

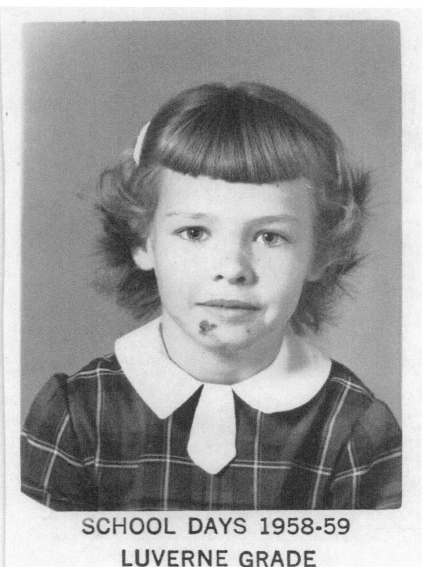

SCHOOL DAYS 1958-59
LUVERNE GRADE

*to hideous 1st grade picture.*

*Horn Shelter*

*Monk and me*

*Standing:*
*Mama Horn, Aunt Glenda & Uncle Green Horn, Daddy,*
*Mother holding me, Mae Brook, Pappy*
*Seated:*
*Cousin Bess & Jack Horn*

*Pappy and me*

*my TSU graduation with cousin Bess Horn*

*me, Dinah, Delwin and Genevieve*

*Nealy Inez Massey Rogers & Daniel Laxey Rogers*
*(Danny's parents)*

*our wedding day*

# Chapter Fourteen

## *College*

*"It isn't where you came from. It's where you're going that counts."* - Ella Fitzgetald

College was not fun. Since Mama would not let me go to Carraway like Dinah and Genny were allowed to do, and Danny and Mama teamed up to convince me to not leave town, I opted to attend Troy State University. I wasn't even allowed to live on campus. I was a commuter.

Shortly after graduation from Luverne High School I participated in freshman orientation at TSU. I came home with a financial aid packet. Daddy took one look at it, handed it back to me, and his exact words were, "Hell no! I ain't filling that thing out. It ain't nobody's damn business what I make." I was blessed that Daddy paid for college, even after we were married. I was the first in my immediate family to earn a four year college degree.

When fall quarter registration began I learned that those of us who attended summer quarter had to be the last ones to register. I thought that was an unusual penalty and grumbled about it aloud one day. Another student informed me that if I got a job working at registration

I could register first every quarter. I soon made that happen. It was about mid quarter before I learned I was in the wrong economics class. I was glad to pull a C in that class with Nick Cervera as the instructor. Registering last that fall quarter meant very few electives were available. I felt like a fish out of water in the French class I took. I had never had a day of any foreign language in my life.

However, because I had no social life at college I finished at age 20 in three years. I never stayed out a single quarter. I got classes as early as I could then drove the 20 miles home to work in the afternoons. I had to use Mama's car to make that commute. Some days others from Luverne and I managed to carpool.

The summer of 1971, as I was focused on bridal showers and a wedding, I took a 7:00 a.m. geography class. The professor would turn off the lights, turn on the slides, and speak in a boring monotone voice. My eyelids were as heavy as lead as I tried really hard to stay awake. That was the only course I made a D in during college. When I play Trivial Pursuit I try to avoid the geography category.

I graduated from Troy State University with a BS degree in Elementary Education. That was probably the proudest day in the lives of both my parents.

# Chapter Fifteen
## Marriage

*"A good marriage is one which allows for change and growth in the individuals and in the way they express their love."*
- Pearl S. Buck

When we were dating, Danny told me he loved me long before I said those words in return. His proposal was anything but romantic. No photographer hidden in the bushes. No rose petals. No champagne. Christmas of 1970 he gave me my ring as a Christmas gift in front of his parents and sister. I'm not even sure he got down on one knee. We were so poor he had to borrow his daddy's credit card to purchase my ring at Service Merchandise in Montgomery with the understanding he would pay back the money. There was no concern about carats, clarity, cut, or color. We set a wedding date for September 12, 1971, the day before I turned 19. I had completed five quarters at TSU.

I'm glad that while we were going steady and engaged the walls of the jail office could not talk. That is where we stopped each night as Danny left the jail to share a good night kiss and a little caressing.

## Marriage

Mama's sewing machine was in my bedroom at the jail. In her spare time, she made my wedding dress, most of my five attendants' dresses, and the flower girl's dress. She also made her mother of the bride dress.

Daddy offered us $500.00 to elope. He always said he didn't want to give me away because he might have to take me back. The biggest expense was our photographer, Mike Lisenby. I still treasure our wedding photo album. Daddy's sense of humor emerged when he asked Mike to take a picture of himself, Pastor Charles Sims, and Danny standing in the church with an open empty wallet.

So on Sunday afternoon September 12, 1971, Danny and I spoke vows to each other. Every pew of Luverne First Baptist Church was filled. Our reception was in the fellowship hall. My sister, Dinah, presided over the registration book. My sister, Genny, was my matron of honor. Mother made the 4-tiered wedding cake and Kathryn Tomlin assembled and decorated it.

After about an hour and a half of hugging in a receiving line, cutting the cake, drinking punch, and mingling with friends and family, Danny found me and whispered, "Can we get out of here?"

Danny's mother, Nealey Rogers, was a wonderful seamstress. She made my going away dress of peach crepe fabric with brown smocking at the waist. She also made Danny's navy sport coat he wore as we exited the church. I threw my bouquet and he tossed the garter as we dodged rice being thrown and ran to his white car. It had been written all over and shaving cream adorned the black top and windshield. We began our trek to the Pensacola, Florida area for our three night honeymoon.

*Breaking Out of an Alabama Jail!*

Danny seldom expresses his love with flowers and chocolate. He details my car. I mean wash, wax, vacuum - a full detail job. He knows how much and why I despise to wash a vehicle. A small but significant way he demonstrates his love for me is always letting me have the last Cheez-It in the package or the last sip of Mountain Dew Zero we might be sharing.

I seem to express my love for him with food. I enjoy baking a cream cheese pound cake and serving him a warm piece with a glass of cold milk. And I always share the extra frosting from a homemade German chocolate cake. He reminds me to let him "sop the bowl" and lick the beaters.

Have we changed and grown as individuals? You bet. Is marriage hard? Yes, it is. Is the effort worth it? Absolutely!

# Chapter Sixteen

## Honeymoon from Hell

*"Love does not consist of gazing at each other, but in looking together in the same direction."*- Antoine

We looked in the same direction as we anticipated our wedding night at the Tiki House on Pensacola Beach. Somehow Danny paid for that night. The other two nights we stayed in some small motel in Gulf Breeze that we had earned by listening to a sales presentation a few months prior to September.

We ate at a restaurant called Butler's. I ordered fried chicken. Danny ordered meat loaf. We walked on the beach. Remember, I went from Mama to marriage so I stalled for about 45 minutes in the bathroom of the "honeymoon suite". The Tiki House honeymoon suite was just a basic room that happened to be at the end of the second floor. The bed had a rattan headboard. As the wedding night activities commenced, I got my teased hair hung in that headboard.

Danny's white car had been written on from one end to the other. We spent practically the whole first day of our honeymoon washing, waxing, and detailing that car.

You can imagine how exciting and romantic that was. We carved out a couple of hours to relax and enjoy the beach.

On Tuesday we explored downtown Pensacola. At lunchtime we walked into a restaurant and soon realized there was no way we could afford a meal, let alone two meals. After whispering about how we were going to tactfully handle this situation, we ordered one dessert and water. Living off of love is real!

We drove home on Wednesday in a spotless car to resume work and school. The basement of the Crenshaw County Jail became our home for the next nine months.

# Chapter Seventeen

## My Mother, the Sheriff's Wife

*"But you are a chosen people, a royal priesthood, a holy nation, a people belonging to God, that you may declare the praises of Him who called you out of darkness into His wonderful light."* 1 Peter 2:9 (NIV)

It was a late cool autumn night when the woman was brought in a drunken stupor to the Crenshaw County, Alabama jail. Her three year old accompanied her because she couldn't be left alone at the place where her mother was arrested. While the frightened child's mom was being fingerprinted and booked, the kind-hearted sheriff's wife took the child into the kitchen, cuddled her in her lap, and satisfied her confused heart and mind with hugs, and filled her empty tummy with homemade gingerbread and milk. Later that night a county social worker came and took the little girl away. Where the grace of Christ needed to be made real that particular night it was. And when that child needed someone to stand in the gap my mother was there. I have seen my mother over and over be the shining light to those in a dark place.

## My Mother, the Sheriff's Wife

The food allowance for the prisoners only covered two meals per day so Mama would make gingerbread in the early evening. Warm large portions of that treat with milk were served to the prisoners for their supper. Mama's belief was nobody went to bed on an empty stomach.

*The Andy Griffith Show* had a character named Otis Campbell who showed up regularly at the jail. We had an "Otis" who showed up many weekends, arrested for public drunkenness. He knew he could get a warm place to sleep and Mama's good food three times a day.

As a young girl, I watched Mama invite a female prisoner to sit outside in the fresh air and sunshine. The woman was nursing her baby so she was allowed to have the baby with her in jail. Check forgery was the charge against the woman. This particular prisoner was housed in an individual cell. When Mama would unlock her cell and escort her to the side yard I got to play with a real baby instead of a baby doll.

Somehow with all her other obligations, Mama had a daycare in the large basement of the jail. This didn't affect us because with college and work we were basically only there at night. And we had no kitchen so we ate upstairs with Mama and Daddy.

Mother began keeping Tammy at six weeks old. Tammy's mom was a hard-working single mother of five. Tammy became the little sister I never had. She was my flower girl in our wedding. Many years later our daughter, Erin, was a junior bridesmaid in Tammy's wedding. Tammy is now a grandmother of two precious boys. Isn't life interesting?

### Breaking Out of an Alabama Jail!

My mother gave her best and almost her life on Sunday night July 25, 1971. A man rang the doorbell of the jail. Mama left Daddy in the living room and went to answer the doorbell. The man who stood there stuck a shotgun in Mama's chest. He had no idea the person he was facing.

Mama grabbed the barrel of the gun and it hit the floor. The man knocked Mama to the floor and began choking her. The jailer (perhaps a hired worker or a trustee prisoner) had just started up the stairs. Mr. Hughes raced back downstairs and struck 20-year-old Randy Sport across the head with a heavy ring of keys. Sport bolted out the door and sped away in his car. Mama was hospitalized with bruises, abrasions, and an ankle injury that required a cast.

Sport was later arrested at the home of his father. He was jailed on charges of assault with intent to murder, unlawful possession of a firearm, and aiding a convict to escape. He did not succeed in the attempted jailbreak of his buddy. Instead, he became a fellow inmate.

Danny and I were on a date visiting friends that night so as soon as we returned home and learned what had happened we raced to the hospital.

On April 18, 1985 at age 68 my mother succumbed to a cancerous brain tumor. Switching roles with her and becoming the caretaker and decision maker has been the hardest thing I have done so far in my life. I slipped her ring from her finger and passed it on to Tammy as Mama had requested. After her death, I received a letter from a good friend. She compared my mother to Dorcas. Acts 9:36 tells us *"in Joppa there was a disciple named*

### My Mother, the Sheriff's Wife

*Tabitha (which, when translated, is Dorcas) who was always doing good and helping the poor."* That was my mother, Guyneese Horn, the sheriff's wife.

# Chapter Eighteen

## My Daddy, the Sheriff

*"When my father didn't have my hand, he had my back."*- Linda Poindexter

My paternal grandfather, Lennie Franklin Horn, was elected sheriff of Crenshaw County in 1938, 1942, and 1946. In 1942 he was the only person to ever run unopposed for that position. After Papa Horn's death in 1947, his son, Green Horn, was appointed to serve the unexpired term. Ray M. Horn, my daddy, was elected sheriff in 1950. From that time until 1972 there was only one term when he was not sheriff. Basil Kennedy was elected in 1954.

Daddy reminded me of our 36th president of the United States, Lyndon B. Johnson. He was large in stature, had sizeable ears, and a similar hairline like LBJ. Ray Horn never met a stranger. He could hobknob with a farmer in overalls or a bank president in a three-piece suit. Daddy kept his right hand on the top of his steering wheel and threw up two fingers at every person he met, even if he was in California. He didn't want to be accused of being unfriendly, especially if he was waving to a potential voter.

## My Daddy, the Sheriff

Daddy and Mama went to every viewing at Turner's Funeral Home. That was just part of being a public official. I often had to accompany them. We would return to our car and Mama would say, "He/she looked so natural, just like he/she should speak." My response would be, "He/she looked like wax. Do not have an open casket at my funeral!"

When Daddy arrested someone with liquor on their person it was confiscated and placed for evidence in the vault in the office of the jail. When a bootlegger's whiskey still was destroyed the liquor was brought in stored in a demijohn bottle. Those glass bottles were large with a narrow neck. The few times I happened to be in the office when the vault door was opened the odor was rank.

Daddy referred to me as his "top crop." Once when shopping with Daddy in Montgomery for a piano, I was with one of the salesmen, across the showroom from Daddy. The salesman asked if Sheriff Horn was my granddaddy. Those large ears perked up and Daddy quickly replied, "I'm her daddy and she's my top crop."

Daddy enjoyed taking my friends and me to various places. Almost anytime he took me to an Alabama football game at Legion Field in Birmingham one of my girlfriends got to tag along. I think I was in high school when I realized college football games had a 4th quarter. Determined to beat the crowd, Daddy would file us out at the end of the third quarter and be as far south as Alabaster before the final down was played. Daddy drove fast and scared the bejeezus out of us.

Daddy would load up three or four girls, and accompany us to Garrett Coliseum in Montgomery, to enjoy Big Bam shows. WBAM, a radio station in Montgomery, hosted many current stars of the 1950s and 1960s. Daddy would let us girls sit together and he would climb up into the nosebleed section. We got to feel grown-up but he kept his eyes on us. We heard such stars as The Dave Clark Five, Paul & Paula, Lightnin' Lou Christie and many more.

One rainy evening Daddy was driving us cheerleaders to Brundidge, Alabama to a basketball game. As we approached the intersection in the community of Springhill Daddy hit the brakes and we began skidding. Calmly, in that slow Southern drawl he said, "Hold on, girls. I've done this before." The car slid across the road, turned up on its left side, came back down to rest, and missed the chimney of a house by just a few feet. The people in the house let Daddy call my brother. Delwin and Uncle Henry came to our rescue and we made it a little late to the game to cheer.

In June of 1972, the Horn sheriff dynasty came to a sad end. Daddy was one of twelve men indicted by a federal grand jury on charges of conspiracy to operate an illegal gambling business. Daddy called a meeting in the living room of the jail which included my mother, Deputies Horn and Clements, Daddy's secretary, Agnes Pynes, and our pastor, Charles Sims. Daddy told the group he had been falsely accused. Daddy also told those affected that he knew the U.S. District Judge, Frank M. Johnson, and could not, at age 64, risk going before him and being imprisoned. So Daddy tendered his resignation. Under Alabama law Crenshaw County Coroner, Joe Smith, became sheriff, pending an appointment by the governor's office.

## *My Daddy, the Sheriff*

Daddy passed away from cancer on September 9, 1976, at age 68.

# Chapter Nineteen

## Infertility, or Playing God?

*"Let your hopes, not your hurts, shape your future."-*
Robert H. Schuller

More than wanting to be a nurse and more than wanting to be a teacher, I wanted to be a mom. So after my teaching career began I stopped my birth control pills and calculated when I would have to get pregnant to have a baby during the summer months. When that didn't happen I would go back on the pill.

Once I had taught for three years and signed my fourth contract, I attained tenure. Feeling that my job was secure, we decided I would get off birth control and stay off. After a year or so of not getting pregnant, I discussed options with my ob/gyn, Dr. Perry. Temperature charts were no fun. Biopsies hurt. Clomid was expensive. Danny even saw a urologist. So with my endometriosis and his low sperm count we were unlikely to conceive.

After hearing Danny's urologist suggest that we might consider adoption, we did just that. We contacted Crenshaw County Welfare Department (Human Resources) and were assigned a case worker, Jeri Ellison. Pages of paperwork had to be filled out. Many questions had to be answered. Interviews and home visits were required. A budget had to be submitted showing we had at least $100.00 left over after meeting monthly expenses. We waited and waited. Each month brought disappointment when I realized I wasn't pregnant, nor had we received the call about the baby we desperately wanted to adopt.

A few weeks after the 1977-78 school year began I experienced a tiredness like I had never felt before. I also noticed some unusual changes in my body. One day while the students were out of the room I put my head down on my desk. A colleague passed by, stuck her head in the door, and asked if I was alright. I told her I had never felt so fatigued. She commented, "I bet you are pregnant."

I did an at-home pregnancy test but was having trouble believing it was positive. My friend, Pam Perdue, was a nurse at the health department. She told me to meet her there early one morning. After a urine test, she confirmed the good news. I needed one more confirmation so as quickly as I could get an appointment I saw Dr. Perry in Montgomery. When I heard the news I hugged his neck. He calculated my due date for June 22. My quick response was , "My mother's birthday is June 24." So he said, "Okay, let's say June 24 then."

We did request to stay on the adoption list throughout the pregnancy. We knew if a miscarriage occurred we didn't want to start over with that process.

Erin Rebecca Rogers was born June 11, 1978, at 10:21 p.m. at St. Margaret's Hospital in Montgomery, Alabama. God's perfect timing!

# Chapter Twenty

## Our Five-Decade Love Story

*"The greatest marriages are built on teamwork, a mutual respect, a healthy dose of admiration, and a never-ending portion of love and grace."*- Fawn Weaver

As we approached our 50th wedding anniversary on September 12, 2021, I began to think about five decades of our lives together. I had enjoyed Pat Perdue Davis taking us through their 50 years of marriage on Facebook so, with her permission, I decided to do the same thing. The following pages have been changed somewhat from what I posted on Facebook in 2021 so as not to repeat too much but still captures our lives together through sickness and health, for richer or poorer, and all that comes in between.

### 1971-1981

We got married the day before I turned 19 and I'm sure tongues in Luverne were wagging but I was not pregnant. My mother made my wedding gown and I thought it was beautiful. She probably spent $25.00 on the white satin and lace. In my spare time, while working at Edna Ruth's

Cloth Shop, I would sit on a stool and sew tiny seed pearls on the lace that trimmed the neckline and sleeves.

After we had to vacate the basement of the Crenshaw County Jail we moved into the tiny downstairs furnished apartment at Mrs. Ruby Crenshaw's on Highway 331 where we paid $25.00 a month. Later we moved to the larger upstairs apartment of Mrs. Crenshaw's home and paid $35.00 a month. Daddy was sorry that we had to move from the basement and bought us a refrigerator for that apartment. How I hated going to the laundromat and lugging a heavy basket of clothes up those steep stairs!

While I commuted to Troy for three years Danny worked because we needed to eat and pay rent. He had attended Lurleen B. Wallace Junior College in Andalusia, Alabama on a baseball scholarship. When I got my job teaching at Luverne Elementary in 1973, we bought a brand new 12 x 60 mobile home - the only home we've ever lived in that was not someone else's before us.- I often laugh and tell friends we're still married because we never went through the process of building a house together. After Daddy's death in September of 1976 we sold the trailer and moved in with Mama for a while.

As Danny and I matured together, we came to the realization that God was in control, not us. We brought our much loved and long awaited daughter home to our house on East Third Street, known as the Martin House. It had large rooms, tall ceilings, no central heating and a/c, but was filled with love. We loved the evenings when I got home from teaching and Danny got home from Super Foods and we were a family of 3. Little did we know Danny's mother, Nealey Rogers, would only have 13 months with Erin. We lost her to cancer in July of 1979.

*Breaking Out of an Alabama Jail!*

In 1980 I was elected to the Luverne City Council, the first female to hold that position. That was certainly a learning experience. One afternoon after three year old Erin and I got home she looked up at me and asked, "Mommy, where do you have to go tonight?" I told Danny that night that one term on the city council with many night meetings and an occasional out of town conference was enough while trying to raise a child.

Erin thrived at her Nana's daycare and loved all her little friends.

## 1981-1991

A strong marriage endures triumphs and tragedies. We certainly had both the second decade of our marriage. I had worked hard to earn my M.Ed from Auburn University Montgomery (AUM) from 1976-1979 while working full time and having a baby. Danny had begun a good job at Pepsi of Luverne where he was moving into management positions - warehouse, operations, etc. He was encouraged to go back to college and finish his degree. He worked full time and went to Troy StateUniversity at Montgomery at night and earned his BS degree in 1982.

Mother valiantly fought a brain tumor. One night Erin was spending the night with her Nana and called to tell us Nana could not remember how to get out of the bathtub. We rushed the short distance to her house and we could tell Mama was so embarrassed that Danny had to help her out of the tub. After that incident, Dr. Pat Walker told us she could not live by herself any longer. We were so proud of Erin for being brave and handling calling us and unlocking the back door as a six year old. So Mama came to live with us. Hiring and firing sitters was difficult. When Mama was hospitalized I would stay all night with her. Danny would bring Erin by the hospital to see her Nana on his way to work. Erin and I would get breakfast at Hardee's then go to school. I graded many papers of third grade students while sitting at my mother's bedside. In April of 1985 Mama met Jesus face to face.

That same year in November, Danny's daddy passed away suddenly. Erin was a second grader with no living grandparents. That's when Danny's sister, Jeanice, stepped in and filled the gap, doting on Erin every chance she got.

Danny continued to work hard and became general manager of Pepsi. He was in a high pressure job some days but he enjoyed great perks like golf outings, flying with the TSU football team to Miami, conventions in great cities, a company car, etc. He even won a Club Med vacation to Eleuthera where Erin learned to water ski and soar on the flying trapeze. In 1991 Danny was called on a Saturday morning to go to his office. He came home a broken man having lost his job. When Danny started seeking jobs in the bottling industry in other states Erin quickly announced,"Y'all can move if you want to. I'm gong to find me a friend who will let me move in with her. I'm not going anywhere!" I'm sure Patsy and Bobby Owens were hoping we didn't leave Luverne or they would have a fourth daughter to raise.

# Breaking Out of an Alabama Jail!
## 1991-2001

This was for sure an eventful decade mostly centered around Erin and her activities. Erin was in the LHS marching band and concert band. Her junior year the concert band was invited to play in Carnegie Hall. Danny was able to make that trip with her. She participated in beauty pageants and was an attendant her senior year in the homecomig court.

I returned to AUM and earned my Educational Leadership certificate so the last four years in education at Luvene School (K-12) I was an assistant principal. I was the first female in administration in the Crenshaw County School System. Erin graduated third in her class and I was honored to get to hand her diploma to her along with a big hug.

Erin attended Troy University. The one time I lived vicariously through her was getting her set up in a mobile home in Dozier Trailer Park with her friends Jessica and Haley. I enjoyed decorating her bedroom and bathroom. I knew she was about to have an experience which I was denied. Erin participated in a sorority for a couple of years but moved home once she got into the nursing program so she could better focus on her studies. I didn't see the top of our dining table for a year and a half since it was covered with paperwork and heavy thick textbooks.

Danny was working hard but took time off to have Dr. Steve Nichols, a high school classmate of mine, operate on his knee that was injured during football in the 1960s. That's when Danny began cycling for rehabilitation and it has remained his passion. On September 11, 2001, we were vacationing at Earl and Carol Franks' townhouse in

Panama City Beach. Danny and I were riding our bicycles on Front Beach Road near Edgewater Beach Resort. Danny had a radio on his bike and we heard the fateful news of a plane crashing into one of the Twin Towers in New York City. When we heard that the second tower had been hit we knew it wasn't an accident and rushed back to the townhouse and turned on the news. We woke Erin and Jeanice and watched in horror, not realizing how those events would change the world.

## 2001-2011

This was a decade of changes for our family. Most were good. Some were not. So much happened during this period that I decided to just make a list.

- July 2003 we became grandparents to Cole. What a blessing!

- June 2004 we took a leap of faith and moved to Panama City Beach into a double wide in a retirement community. I believe I would have lived in a cardboard box under the Hathaway Bridge if it meant getting closer to that grandson.

- June 2004 I was hired as an intervention specialist with Community Intervention and Research Center. We invested in sixty-eight candy machines and placed those in various locations around the county. This was a huge financial mistake on our part.

- December 2004 CIRC management called all employees to the office and told us they were closing the doors. I lost my job. The four-sided candy machines in which one could drop a quarter to get a handful of sweet treats were not doing well. We had two mortgages and two power bills because the house in Luverne had not sold. Once again we learned that God was in control and knew the plans and big picture for us.

• 2005 Danny went to work with Advantage Sales and Marketing as a Gatorade and Tropicana sales rep. I went back into the classroom at Merriam Cherry Street Elementary. Isn't life interesting?

• April 24, 2006, Anslee was born. We were so excited to have a granddaughter.

• Danny continued to drive back to Luverne on Friday nights to announce home LHS football games as "The Voice of the Tigers" (for 30+years). One Friday night there was a wonderful presentation and the press box was named the Danny C. Rogers Press Box.

• 2007 I went on a Walk to Emmaus at Blue Lake near Andalusia, Alabama. I learned to begin living a life of servanthood for my Lord and Savior.

• Danny was able to partially retire and worked three afternoons a week at Bay Cycle & Fitness with Dallas Smalley. This was a perfect fit for Danny. Since moving to Bay County, Danny had become an avid cyclist. He met a lot of fellow cyclists who became good friends.

## 2011-2021

For the most part this decade was a busy one and a productive one. We moved our membership from Woodlawn Methodist to First United Methodist since we had moved to The Cove area of Panama City and were close in proximity to that church. I retired from education at the end of the 2013-14 school year. After a year off, I began as a substitute teacher at North Bay Haven Charter Academy where both grandchildren were students. This was convenient when I had pick-up duty in the afternoons. I also enjoyed subbing at Holy Nativity Episcopal School. That building reminded me so much of Luverne School. The inside with the shiny hardwood floors even smelled the same as my school where I spent so many precious years of my life as a student and a teacher.

In January 2017, Danny had a very serious bicycle crash and was life-flighted to Tallahassee Memorial Healthcare. Danny spent a week there. Dr. Hank Hutchinson was his surgeon and one of the best in the southeast. Danny was then transferred to Health South in Panama City where he spent two weeks in rehab. The first day he was taken to a physical therapy session he couldn't even lift his left foot off of the floor. Two weeks later he walked out of that facility and was back on his bicycle in April.

We have enjoyed several trips. An Alaskan cruise was the highlight of our travels this decade. There are many places in the United States I want to visit. I'd like to experience Boston, San Antonio, Wyoming, Colorado, and New England. One of my expensive bucket list items is to see Italy. I want to view the architecture, eat the food, and taste the wine.

2018 was one of the most difficult years of our marriage. In May I had a total replacement of my right knee. Rehab at Health Plex was not fun but proved to be just where I needed to be. On the afternoon of October 10 we survived Hurricane Michael, a category 5. We opted to not evacuate. When the wind blew the pounding rain into our fourth floor bayside condo we grabbed every towel and beach towel we owned to soak up the water. I sat in the bathtub and prayed. When I felt the seven story building sway just a bit I prayed, "Lord, let them find our bodies under this rubble!" After three hours of not really knowing what was happening outside, we looked out on the parking lot to see water running in and running up Cherry Street like a river. We lost my van, Danny's truck, and Danny's 1997 Corvette. In December, after a routine mammogram and follow-up ultrasound, I was told I had stage 1 breast cancer. A lumpectomy was performed by Dr. George Reiss. After healing from the surgey, I underwent thirty-three radiation treatments. On March 15, 2019, I rang the bell indicating I was cancer free. The best thing about having breast cancer in the winter months was being told to not wear a bra! I wore lots of vests and scarves.

Only once during this fifty year period did I get mad enough to pack my bag and leave. I have no idea what I was upset about. I went to Erin's and about 2 hours later when she informed me that I was putting her at the center of this squabble I picked up my bag and went home. On September 12, 2021, we celebrated fifty years of marriage. And on September 13, 2021, I turned 69 having lived longer than either of my parents. They died 8 1/2 years apart both at age 68.

# Chapter Twenty-one

## *Every Small Town Needs a Hero*

*"Poetry is a way of taking life by the throat."*
- Robert Frost

Poetry seems to help me cope with various feelings. After Danny's job loss at Pepsi I wrote a poem from Erin's point of view. It was published in a book entitled *Carrying the Torch - The International Library of Poetry.* Just so you know, anyone could have a poem published as long as they bought the book!

### *Every Small Town Needs a Hero*

I've always heard life isn't fair
And now I understand.
When things go wrong or things go right
We must believe God has a plan.

You taught me to know right from wrong
And to hold my head up high.
Now you must do the same, you see
Oh, Daddy, please don't cry.

*Every Small Town Needs a Hero*
Losing your job was so unfair
To our whole family.
But we'll do what we have to do
And it'll work out, you'll see.

I know you'll search with all your might
'Til a new job can be found.
But I just thought you'd like to know
It's nice having you around.

Don't worry, Daddy, I'll stand beside you
And everything will be just fine.
'Cause every small town needs a hero
And I'm so glad you're mine!

I treasure this piece written by Erin when she was in junior high school. It has no title.

When I think of my mother,
I think of
The scent of potpourri spreading
Throughout the house,
Chocolate chip cookies
Baking in the oven
Blooming flowers in the garden,
I hear her
Baking in the kitchen,
Playing the piano,
Stirring around early in the morning,
I see her

*Breaking Out of an Alabama Jail!*
Expressing her friendliness to everyone,
Reading a book,
Caring for those she loves most,
I feel
Her grief when she's sad,
Her warmth when she's happy,
Our closeness when we're together.

# Chapter Twenty-two

## Special Memories

*"Grandparents can be very special resources. Just being close to them reassures a child, without words, about change and continuity, about what went before and what will come after."*- Fred Rogers

I've solicited from my nieces, nephews, and daughter fond memories of Mama, Daddy, and visiting them in the jail. Of course, Erin never knew her Papa Horn as he passed away before she was born. With their permission, I'm sharing memories they had of their grandparents.

Mama and Daddy had bought the small white wooden house that stood behind the jail years before Daddy left office. Mama remained in this house after Daddy's death and continued her daycare.

Erin's fondest memories of her Nana were staying at her daycare and all the friends she had there. Jeremy Messick pushed her into the window air conditioning unit and that left a tiny scar on her face. Kate Norman would have a little temper tantrum sitting in her high chair and throw food on the floor. Kimberley Maddox enjoyed playing with a cylinder shaped oatmeal box Mama threw on the floor more than she did a $20.00 toy. Erin's favorite food at Nana's daycare was sloppy Joes. Since Erin was an only child, she loved spending time at her Nana's daycare. She also loved the single attention she got from Mama when she would stay the night with her on Fridays. Their Saturday morning ritual would be to go to Luverne Bank & Trust Company and the grocery store.

Not too many children in the 1960s and early 1970s could go back to school in the fall and write about their summer adventures of visiting their grandparents in the jail. The ones who lived away from Luverne would often spend one or two weeks with Mama and Daddy.

### Nina Hudson McGinnis

Nina, Dinah's daughter, was the oldest granddaughter and the only one of Dinah's three children who would come and stay without her parents. She remembers the bats at dusk flying around the car dealership across the street and sometimes coming into our space where we were playing in the yard. She remembers her Grandmama making new clothes for her while she was visiting.

### Madge Hudson Sims

Madge was Dinah's youngest but never came to stay a week at the time like her sister. She did remember when she was at the jail visiting with her mother and daddy standing at the foot of the steep stairs that led up to the jail. She told me she remembered thinking *I've never seen what it looks like up there. I could just sneak up there and take a look and nobody would ever know.* She never did get up the courage to do that.

Dinah's son, Al, never came for a visit by himself either. Al is the only one of my parents' grandchildren that is now deceased.

<u>Willie Ray Horn</u>

I remember a trustee at the jail that let me walk to town with him to get various items for the prisoners. He held my hand in his to keep me from running across the street.

One time I slipped while swinging from a rail at the top of the outside stairs. I hit my head and the trustee picked me up and took me to the hospital. The hospital was where the Luverne Health and Rehabilitation is today.

We ate watermelon and Wade put salt on his which I thought was weird.

Men barbequed on a homemade cinder block grill pit in the backyard. They cooked goat and I thought the more you chewed the bigger it got.

When I was at the jail in the afternoons Darlin' let me ride with her to take Monk home.

Christmas and Thanksgiving were always so special. The food was abundant and delicious. The adults ate at the dining table and the kids ate in the kitchen.

Darlin' had one of those silver aluminum Christmas trees. A color wheel sat on the floor a few feet from it. When the wheel was turned on and started to spin the tree would change colors.

On the hallway wall before entering the living room, Darlin' strung rows of string at Christmas time and that's where their Christmas cards were displayed.

One day Becky was not around and Darlin' had me stand on an ottoman in the living room. She slipped a dress she was making for Becky on me so she could get the correct hem length. I guess Becky and I were about the same height at that time. I was surely hoping nobody walked in on that.

Becky and I played in the walk in storage closet in the hallway across from the kitchen. She had a plastic cow on wheels with a stick handle attached to its head. Becky would lift the handle and the cow would let out a loud "moo" that would scare the living daylights out of me every time.

Every birthday while growing up I received a card with $2 in it from Darlin' and Papa Horn.

Papa Horn was the most neatly dressed man I knew. I aspired to be a meticulous dresser like him.

Genevieve's boys, Wade and Tim, shared lots of memories of their time spent with their Papa Horn and Darlin'.

# *Breaking Out of an Alabama Jail!*
## Wade Weaver

I remember riding with Papa Horn and he would raise two fingers on the top of the steering wheel to wave at each car we met. I asked him "Papa Horn, do you know all these people you are waving to?" He said,"If I don't know them, I know who they belong to." So, as you can imagine, I had to ask who was in every car we passed and he had the answer. I surely couldn't dispute any of his answers.

I remember all of the beds in the basement of the jail and how our families could all sleep there at once.

I remember one Thanksgiving when Darlin' and Papa were living in the house next to the jail. We picked up pecans all day Friday. About the time we thought we were finished, a man came by on a tractor with an arm on it and Papa Horn paid him to shake all the trees and we started all over. We wanted to shoot the man on the tractor.

I remember all the desserts Darlin' cooked for Thanksgiving and how when we started home she would give me an egg custard to take home. She knew it was my favorite.

I remember Papa Horn always had a watermelon during the season and he would always get it out of the refrigerator before we went to bed. I still love watermelon!

I remember going to the curb market to get boiled peanuts and watermelon. The curb market intrigued me because we just didn't have them in Briminghan.

## Special Memories

I remember when Tim and I went to the Orange Bowl with Darlin', Papa, Becky, and Danny. The first thing that sticks out is we decided to leave about 9 or 10 the night before we had originally planned to leave. The next memory is of Papa getting stopped for speeding in some small town called Clayhatchee and he didn't have his driver's license because he got a new wallet for Christmas and didn't put it in there. An hour or two later, I think Becky said something about hoping our tickets were on the Alabama side of the stadium. This prompted Darlin' to say, "Ray, you did remember to get the tickets?" Then Papa slapped his chest and said, "Oh hell!" We were in south Georgia, maybe Valdosta. We stopped and called Uncle Henry and he and Uncle Delwin met us in I think Andalusia with Papa's license and the tickets. I remember the next morning we stopped in Florida somewhere and I ate a hamburger for breakfast which I thought was great because I had never done that. I remember getting to the game and it was pouring down rain. Tim and I were sitting with Becky and Danny. We were under the upper deck. It was raining so hard you could hardly see the other side of the field. Coach Bryant came out of the locker room in a rain suit. As soon as he opened the gate and stepped on the field, the rain stopped immediately. We got killed in the game but it was a trip I will never forget. I also remember wearing a suit and tie to the game.

I remember a young state trooper who covered Crenshaw County. He wrecked two trooper cars in about a week because he was driving too fast. Papa started calling him Thunderbolt!

I remember us playing football in the front yard of the jail and then later on playing in the side yard at the courthouse.

*Breaking Out of an Alabama Jail!*

I remember returning to the jail after the Horn Reunion the day the first men landed on the moon and watching it on the black and white TV in the living room before we went home.

I remember Monk and all the great meals we had in Luverne.

I remember one time someone asked Papa where he had been and he answered,"All over hell and half of Rutledge." I still say that sometimes and people look at me like I'm crazy.

I remember coming to Luverne to stay for a week or two every summer and one of those weeks was always the week of VBS at First Baptist. I remember Darlin' always taught Vacation Bible School.

I remember Cousin Bess living next door and Pappy living in the basement and visiting with them.

I remember Papa busting a still and bringing those five gallon demi-johns full of moonshine to the jail and pouring them out and Darlin' planting flowers in them.

I remember those times fondly and just think how simple life seemed. The innocence of youth is a wonderful thing!


Tim Weaver

Darlin' had to run an errand so, of course, I had to go with her. Once we arrived she told me to stay in the car. It was summer and very hot so she left the car running with the A/C on.  I saw what I thought was a can of air freshener on the seat.  I sprayed a little into the A/C vent only to find out very quickly that it was not air freshener. It quickly overwhelmed me with my eyes burning and me coughing to no end.  It was mace.  I never did that again. That was the day I learned how to read labels.

Walking with Mother down the street, South Forest Avenue, the business district, the men would step aside and tip their hat and greet her with "howdy do Ms. Genevieve."

I remember the Chicken Shack and the delicious friend chicken.

When a loved one passed away it was customary to have the casket placed in the living room for the family. The city would put traffic cones out that read "Quiet... death in the family."

(author's note:  My daddy's body was brought home for a couple of days and  nights before his funeral.  His open casket was in the living room.  I thought this was morbid but it was Mama's decision and was normal.  I remember Mr. Glenn Handley and Mr. James Morgan sitting up all night with the body.)

I remember curb markets with sawdust floors. Papa loved watermelon.  He would apread the newspaper on a table and cut them.  He always had the best sweetest watermelons.  I love watermelon, sometimes a little too much.  Being in Luverne began an addiction that has followed me my entire life.  The curb market right past the Patsaliga River coming into town had a washtub full of boiled peanuts for sale.  I ate so many they would make me sick. You would think that would teach me a lesson but NO! I still order green peanuts from south Alabama and cook them myself. As a matter of fact, I cook a half bushel and deliver them to my friends in Tennessee. They love me. The market also had a mule that walked around an old sugar cane press. Cane juice was a favorite of mine. I learned the hard way not to drink it before bedtime.

Uncle Roy, Darlin's brother, let me go to work with him on the garbage truck. It was hotter than damn-it! That experience helped move my future aspirations in a different direction.

With Papa being the Sheriff and the jail being upstairs from us many meals were provided to the prisoners. I remember my mother saying she thought men got purposely arrested so they could eat in the Crenshaw County Jail.

We knew early on that you didn't get down from the table unless you ate everything on your plate. One breakfast morning there was something different on the table. I alrady knew I was going for the country ham, sausage, homemade biscuits , and red eye gravy. I asked about the mystery dish. Papa said it was brains and eggs. I thought the world as I knew it was coming to an end. I sat morionless for what seemed like an hour. I was thinking my grandfather was eating the brains of dead people. Even after finding out what it really was the memory follows me to this day. I laugh about it now.

You better be at the table on time. If you weren't washed and sitting at the table at precisely the right time you might not get to eat. We were playing football on the courthouse lawn. The courthouse bell chimed at noon everyday. I heard the bell start to ring and I immediately knew I had to run to get to the jail in time. I got there late. Papa told me I wasn't going to be able to have dinner (lunch) and that I would have to wait until supper. I was heartbroken and upset. I went in the living room and had a seat. Papa had to go back to work and left for the courthouse. Darlin' came in and said, "You know when to be here for meals?" I answered, "Yes ma'am." She said, "You come with me." I followed her into the kitchen and she fixed me a plate of food. She told me ,"Don't you say anything to your Papa about this. Do you hear me?" I again answered, "Yes ma'am." I learned a little discipline that day.

In the sixties fireworks were not regulated like they are today. We would buy M-80s and cherry bombs. They were so powerful that kids had been known to lose fingers and eyes because of them. We would throw them at each other. Let me tell you there were a few close calls. It didn't take long for my mother to put a stop to us throwing them at each other. Little did she know folks across town were losing their mailboxes. We didn't know it was a felony.

Pecans, pecans, pecans! They were everywhere. Papa would tell us to go down and pick them up so Darlin' would be able to make some pies. It really wasn't that fun. We would get rakes and try to knock them down. One day a man with a tractor drove down into the pasture to the pecan trees. He wrapped a chain or a strap around the trunk of each pecan tree one at a time. When he got back up on the tractor he engaged the PTO and that pecan tree started to shake which caused hundreds of pecans to start raining down. I was amazed he was able to do that. Then it would dawn on me who would be picking them up.

## Breaking Out of an Alabama Jail!

I loved going to Luverne. Living in Birmingham came with the price of city noise and industrial pollution not to mention our house on 31$^{st}$ Street was straight on the glide path at the airport. Everything was green in south Alabama. That was when I learned why. Kudzu. It grew everywhere and would devour everything in sight if not kept at bay with chemicals. You could cut it all you wanted to but it would grow back overnight.

Uncle Henry was Darlin's brother. Mama took us to Uncle Henry's for a visit and a meal. As we were getting closer, the windows of his house were up and I began to smell something awful. I said, "Mama, what is that smell?" She answered,"Uncle Henry is cooking chitlins." I knew right away I wasn't going to eat.

(author's note: Chitterlings are also known in the south as chitlins. They are the large intestines of hogs. One of the worst smells I have ever endured in my life was the one time my mama boiled chitlins for my Pappy.)

Mama and I were riding through town when I saw a woman standing on the corner. I said,"Oh my goodness!" Mama said, "What's wrong?" I said, "That lady is so ugly." She said, "Tim Weaver it's not nice to say things like that. She can't help what she looks like." After a brief pause, she said, "But she could stay at home, couldn't she?" We both laughed.

In winter the house was warmed with gas radiant heaters. The heaters were turned off at night in case there was a drop in gas pressure which was dangerous. We slept in the bedroom just off the living room. The bed had a feather mattress which would sink in the middle. Darlin' and Mother would put three or four quilts on us to keep us warm. By morning it was so cold you could see your breath. The smell of Darlin' cooking breakfast was our signal to throw off the covers and run to the kitchen.

Papa Horn took us to the county lake to go fishing. We used cane poles and crickets for bait. Papa used a fly rod and wore waders to get away from the bank. He was catching a bunch and was putting the fish on a stringer and let them trail behind him as he continued to fish. Thinking he had caught enough to have a fish fry, he turned and headed back to get out of the water. When he pulled up the stringer to admire his catch he realized he had been feeding the turtles. They had eaten on a bunch of them. I had never heard my Papa cuss. I did that day.

When folks passed away it was customary to have the casket placed in the room closest to the front of the house. Signs were put out in the street that would read"Quiet... death in the family."

We loved going to Uncle Brown's home. He was my biological maternal grandmother's brother, the grandmother that was killed in a wreck when my mother was a child. There was always something to get into there. We would play in the barn and take turns diving into the corn crib. The billy goat did not like us trying to ride him though. We learned pretty quickly that he wan't having any of it.

Near Uncle Delwin's house there was what I thought was an underground storm shelter. We would go down there and play. It was dark and cool. That was a good thing in the searing humid heat of south Alabama. I did not understand what all the signs meant on the door. Only later did I find out they indicated nuclear fallout shelter.

I'm glad I did not know what was going on in the country and what sat ninety miles off the coast of Florida.

Before we could go to the Luverne pool we had to shell peas and butterbeans. Darlin' would give us porcelain pans and a grocery bag full of peas. We couldn't go swimming until we completed the process. I did not like shelling peas then. I certainly didn't complain though when it came to eating them. I look back fondly to those days. A simple time when you could go anywhere and never have to worry. I think being Ray M. Horn's grandson probably gave us a sense of security. I would give almost anything to be able now to sit on the porch and shell peas with Darlin'.

Playing at night was always an adventure. On a clear night you could see all the stars in the sky. It was so beautiful. We took it for granted and thought everybody had access to its beauty. They did not and that's what was so special about it. For some reason I remember there were a lot of bats that would swoop down and come inches away from our faces. I think I face planted into a swing set trying to dodge them.

We would get a bag and explore all around town. We were in search of Coke botles. I'm sure people thought we were doing good deeds by picking up trash. Nah, we were in it for the money. The deposit on the bottles helped us make money to go to the pool and to buy fireworks.

I remember Darlin' drinking scalding hot coffee from a saucer.

# Chapter Twenty-three
# My Cup Overflows

*"I know what it is to be in need, and I know what it is to have plenty. I have learned the secret of being content in any and every situation, whether well fed or hungry, whether living in plenty or in want. I can do everything through Him who gives me strength."*
Philippians 4:12-13 (NIV)

## Drinking From the Saucer
by John Paul Moore

I've never made a fortune,
And I'll never make one now
But it really doesn't matter
'Cause I'm happy anyhow.

As I go along my journey
I'm reaping better than I've sowed
I'm driking from the saucer
'Cause my cup has overflowed.

I don't have a lot of riches,
And sometimes the going's tough
But with kin and friends to love me
I think I'm rich enough.

*My Cup Overflows*
I thank God for the blessings
That His mercy has bestowed
I'm drinking from the saucer
'Cause my cup has overflowed.

He gives me strength and courage
When the way grows steep and rough
I'll not ask for other blessings for
I'm already blessed enough.

May we never be too busy
To help bear another's load
Then we'll all be drinking from the saucer
When our cups have overflowed.

When I retired from my teaching career (the second time) in 2014 I received a note from one of my former Luverne third graders, Kim Dixon. Kim penned:
*In life so many people spend years hoping to discover their purpose. Even then many aren't sure. We all want to hope that we did something for which we will be remembered or that we somehow made a difference. I pray that you know that not only did you find your purpose in life, you answered your calling. Not only did you make a difference, you changed lives. May God bless this next adventure in your life as you blessed so many through the years.*

He certainly has, Kim, He certainly has!

# Chapter Twenty-four

## Southernese

*"And the Southern girls with the way they talk*
*They knock me out when I'm down there."* - Beach Boys
in the song "California Girls"

Wholla- I heard a blaring siren a wholla go.

Fixinta- I'm fixinta to order food. Want anything?

Fordum- Fourdum three equals twelve.

Y'all- Singular for you all

All y'all- Plural for y'all

Hankerin'- I'm hankerin' for a piece of chocolate cake.

Piddlin'- She was piddlin' in the kitchen when she couldn't sleep.

Fittin'- That fried chicken shore wuz fittin!

Jawl- Jawl see that snake in the road?

Jeet- Jeet supper yet?

Brick bat- What you use to build a brick house

Hose pipe- What you use to water a garden

Hissy fit- Severe temper tantrum

Bless her heart- It's ok to talk about a lady if you bless her heart afterwards.

Plumb crazy- A little more than just crazy

Crazy as a sprayed roach- more crazy than plumb crazy

Gussied up- She got gussied up for Sunday morning church.

Put that in your pipe and smoke it- Think about it (My pappy's favorite)

Dinner- the midday meal in the south

Supper- the nighttime meal in the south

Nem air - Nem air biscuits shore are good.
Translation:Those biscuits surely are good.

# Afterword

*The Crenshaw County Jail no longer stands. The old jail is gone as well as the house my parents owned and moved into after Daddy's resignation. When we go back to Luverne I avoid the street on which they stood. When we lived in the jail Mama had flower beds on both sides of the steps leading up to the front porch. There were mimosa trees and dogwood trees in the front yard. There was no fence with razor wire.*

Made in the USA
Columbia, SC
25 April 2025

57159198R00083